Installing Quality Circles:
A Strategic Approach

Installing Quality Circles: A Strategic Approach

Laurie Fitzgerald
Joseph Murphy

University Associates, Inc.
8517 Production Avenue
P.O. Box 26240
San Diego, CA 92126

Preface

When our interest in the quality-circle (QC) technique was aroused several years ago, it was nearly impossible to find any practical guidelines regarding the installation process. At that time there were television specials that encouraged the use of QCs to improve productivity; there were articles in popular magazines as well as business and human-resource journals that analyzed the advantages and disadvantages of employing the technique; there were hundreds of papers either proclaiming or denying a significant return on investment in QCs; and there were praises of applications in the companies that were experimenting with the concept. In short, a great deal of information and opinion was available, but little instruction of the "how-to" variety could be found.

This situation still exists today, and a number of questions still need to be answered: How does an organization evolve from traditional autocratic and authoritarian management to participative management through quality circles? What important decisions must be made, and how are they made? How is organizational readiness for QCs assessed? What are the risks? How much time is required for implementation? Where does the process begin? How does one "sell" the concept to decision makers? What are the important considerations regarding money, leadership, and training? What are the specific steps involved in installing QCs?

This book was written in an attempt to answer these questions and is based on our experience in implementing and running effective quality-circle programs. We have made and witnessed mistakes, of course, but we have attempted to share them with candor in the hope that our readers may benefit from these experiences and thereby maximize their chances for creating productive quality-circle programs of their own. All of those who become involved in quality circles sooner or later err, but through such errors they progress and grow. In our experience many employees who have not been considered to be valuable assets have turned into "vital cogs," "real leaders," and "key people." This process of learning from mistakes can and should be a valuable and exciting one.

The structure of the book is as follows: Part I provides the reader with a conceptual framework from which to consider QCs. The topics covered include history and definition, budget requirements and structures, advantages and pitfalls, and other information that we believe will be helpful to anyone interested in QCs. Part II contains our model for QC implementation. Each of the nine steps of the model is addressed under the subheadings of *Overview, Content, Participants* (those involved in the process), *Time Frame*, and *Tips for Success*. In Part II we have attempted to exclude unnecessary details and concentrate instead on what is essential to complete each step with confidence. The final part of the book is the Appendix, which provides a QC bibliography.

It is our hope that this book will be used as a guide to a potential-filled adventure into quality circles. Moreover, we believe that the book can help to ensure the success of those readers whose intention is to introduce the profound changes of worker participation into organizations in a strategic manner.

Laurie Fitzgerald
Joseph Murphy

Denver, Colorado
May, 1982

Contents

PART I

THE QUALITY-CIRCLE
PHENOMENON

A Conceptual Framework

DEFINING QUALITY CIRCLES

Although quality circles (QCs) have existed for some twenty years, they are presently enjoying the greatest level of popularity since their inception. Because of the phenomenal way in which they have attracted the interest of American organizations, a number of characteristics and definitions have been associated with them.

Some managers perceive QCs as management tools for eliciting more productivity from reluctant employees; some see them as an answer to declining morale and spirit in the work force; others admit that their intention is to use them to avoid unionism where it threatens. On the other hand, some managers visualize a QC program as one way to move an organization to new levels of participative management, and they see this movement as a natural evolution. Certain groups subscribe to the notion that QCs create and preserve quality in products in order to meet the demands of the consumer, who has become more vocal in recent years. Still others hope that QCs will allow them to maximize the use of resources, especially the untapped brainpower of workers.

There are more perceptions, of course. The point is not to identify each one, but to offer a common denominator as a base on which to build one's own definition. To do so it is necessary to determine the essential elements of a QC: *A quality circle consists of three to twelve employees who perform the same work or share the same work area and function and who meet on a regular basis, normally one hour per week on company time, in order to apply statistical techniques and tools learned in extensive training to problems affecting their work and work area; subsequently, they present solutions and recommendations to their management for the authorization to implement their solutions.*

Additional characteristics should be considered. Most QCs are voluntary and are led by the area supervisor. Also, they are normally coordinated centrally in an organization by a person who has been trained

3

as a facilitator. Finally, QCs are set up with the idea that they will be ongoing.

There are certain things that QCs are not. They are not committees or project teams; they are not meant to deal with organization-wide problems, with compensation or benefit issues, or with grievances; they are not a management tactic designed to disempower an existing union; they are not appointed groups mandating participation in solving management-identified problems; and they are not intended to function on a temporary or intermittent basis.

With all of these factors to consider, it is not surprising that every organization that begins a QC program develops its own unique form and style.

A BRIEF HISTORY OF QUALITY CIRCLES

Quality circles, originally known as quality-control circles or QCCs, have been in use in Japanese industry since 1962. The reason for the development of the technique was simple. The Japanese had recently suffered a devastating defeat at the hands of the Allies. Productive industry in Japan was literally nonexistent. With both financial and technical support from the victors, Japan began to rebuild its industry in an all-out attempt to regain an economic footing in the world market. By 1949 the effort was paying off, and Japanese products were being exported to all points on the globe. All was not well, however. A reputation for product quality was being developed: "Made in Japan" became synonymous with cheap and shoddy merchandise.

The Japanese Union of Scientists and Engineers (JUSE) undertook the task of changing that image. Its members sought a method that could be used in any business to build quality into products. For some time they had recognized the gap between the analysis of work and the work itself, and they decided to bridge that gap by involving employees in the systematic assessment of their own job activities and product quality.

Tools were required for this task, and the person JUSE recruited to develop and teach the use of such tools was an American named W.E. Deming, a statistician whose ideas on quality assurance had fallen on deaf ears in the United States. Deming toured the Japanese islands, lecturing to groups of employees on the value and application of statistical tools in solving quality problems. He was convinced that the Japanese could once again become a world economic force and was not surprised to discover that they readily absorbed his teachings.

Although this account explains the birth of the statistical aspect of QCs, the historical development of their group orientation differs considerably. To explain this development it is necessary to examine the conditions and events of the period following World War I. A national economic boom in Japan had brought about an unprecedented expansion of Japanese industry. The situation seemed ideal for management with the exception of one plaguing problem: Because of the competition developing among companies for the depreciating labor market, workers changed jobs at record rates to obtain the highest possible wages. Eventually the turnover rate reached 52 percent per year.

As an alternative to confronting this problem individually, Japanese business leaders collaborated in the development of a management system that came to be known as "nenko." "Nenko" emphasized the direct recruitment of labor from high schools and farms. The recruiting businesses invested heavily in the specialized training of these inexperienced workers with the purpose of developing skills and knowledge that were applicable only in one industry and, optimally, in one organization.

A second tactic of "nenko" was to incorporate a policy of increasing salaries with length of time spent on the job. Workers, therefore, were underpaid at first and then overpaid as they gained years of one-company employment. The result was that job changing was reduced as employees began to see each day of work as an investment in their financial future. To reinforce this commitment to the company, "nenko" employers guaranteed lifetime employment and decorated the package with many kinds of benefits.

However, recessions developed now and then, forcing the firms to lay off workers. These layoffs and the promise of guaranteed employment would have been contradictory if the dual labor force that currently exists had not come into play. Japanese workers today are of two different types: One group consists of permanent employees who keep their jobs in spite of the economic picture, and the other group comprises temporary workers who come and go with the demand for additional labor. Those who belong to the temporary group include subcontractors and regular workers who have reached the mandatory retirement age of fifty-five but still can be of service to their companies.

What is significant about the development of "nenko," although it involves less than 30 percent of the Japanese work force, is that it produced a way of work in which the group and not the individual determined what was to be done and how. Evaluation, always informal, became dependent on group rather than individual efforts. This process resulted in the practice of collaborative decision making or consensus and was supported by an impressive level of group and company loyalty.

From the combination of statistical techniques and a group orientation toward problem solving came the logical vehicle to carry Japan forward in its growth: quality circles. Throughout the Sixties QCs were initiated and expanded in every sector of the Japanese economy, and the reputation for "shoddy quality" began to be reversed. Many of the products that are now used daily in American life carry the names of Japanese companies. From cars to computers, Japan has become a strong competitor in the world market, often to the consternation of American management and workers. Today five of every six Japanese workers belong to a QC; an estimated two million circles are currently active in Japan, and each member contributes an average of fifty-five suggestions, recommendations, and solutions per year through his or her involvement. In fact, QCs are so extensive in Japan that most companies have annual conferences on the subject. The Japanese Union of Scientists and Engineers sponsors extensive training for facilitators and a series of conventions at which professional papers are presented to the thousands who attend. Quality circles have clearly become a way of organizational life.

It was not until the early Seventies that the QC concept made its way across the Pacific to the shores of the United States. In 1972 a West Coast plant of the Lockheed Aerospace Corporation sent a delegation of managers to Japan to observe their quality-control techniques. These managers were so impressed when they witnessed QCs in action that they returned with an enthusiastic recommendation to senior management to undertake a pilot project. Today the aerospace giant conducts an extensive QC program, and its impressive results have helped spark the interest of other American companies, both large and small.

Success bred success. As QC achievements were communicated throughout the American business world, a movement reminiscent of the gold rush of 1849 ensued. Business leaders like IBM, Reynolds Tobacco, Eastman-Kodak, Martin-Marietta, Hughes Aircraft, Storage Technology Corporation, Hewlett-Packard, Sundstrand, Adolph Coors Company, RCA, and Uniroyal climbed on the bandwagon with their own special styles of quality circles. The 1981 count identified more than 1,200 companies in the United States that were in one stage or another of QC development.

QUALITY CIRCLES: FUNDAMENTAL OR FAD?

The head-turning reaction of business people to the mention of such words as "productivity" or "Japanese management" attests to the widespread desire to learn more about quality circles. At this time in our economic history, the American management audience is hungry for methods to increase output while reducing input. Quality circles appear to be, at first glance, the answer to their hopes, but a word of caution is in order.

Such concepts as zero-based budgeting, management by objectives, sensitivity training, transactional analysis, situational leadership, and matrix organizations have been touted by their proponents as "the answer" to the dilemmas of American business. Each, in its own way, held great potential for contributing to the solutions of the problems that were faced. However, none has delivered all that had been promised. One great idea after another has been rejected and its remnants buried in the storerooms of organizations across the country.

The reasons for this history of rejection are several. Overoptimism and overenthusiasm are chronic characteristics of the American way of life. Misuse or misapplication is a potential contributor, and misunderstanding is certainly a strong factor. In general, the authors feel that the blame lies with the American tendency to adopt a good idea and apply it before spending the proper amount of time required to comprehend it. If it fails, the tendency is to discard it and to try something else.

The controversy that the authors hope to resolve in this part of the book is whether QCs can be expected to become fundamental to American business or whether the concept will find its way, like so many of its predecessors, to the archives of corporations. Perhaps the best way to approach this controversy is to re-examine the Japanese experience with QCs.

After more than twenty years of development in Japan, it can be said unequivocally that quality circles are a fundamental form of organizational life there. Fads tend to begin with an explosion, which is not the case with the progression of QCs in Japan. The intricate, nationwide system of circles that exists today is the result of years of planning, testing, solving, revising, succeeding, and failing. In Japan QCs are evolutionary rather than revolutionary.

The United States has not had a sufficient amount of time to contemplate the QC idea or to let it take root. If QCs are to persist in America, those who are responsible for their installation must be able to proceed with caution, to learn from mistakes, to accept a failure now and then in pursuit of overall success, and to muster the patience to allow pilot circles to flounder until they stabilize.

From the authors' vantage point as consultants for organization development, there is a great deal of evidence that QCs embody a crucial principle of good management: *An involved and respected employee is a productive employee whose work is of the highest quality.* The argument is often raised that the United States achieved the top position in production in the Western world as a result of a long-lasting managerial stance in which employees were viewed solely as pairs of hands. The authors believe that this rise was in spite of, rather than because of, this attitude. Organizational goals, increased competition, consumer demands, and employee needs are leading Americans to a world in which management by participation will be the only management style to survive; and the quality-circle concept is an important stepping stone toward that world.

Therefore, the conclusion proposed by the authors is that QCs specifically and participative management in general are fundamental vehicles in the development of American organizational life. Quality circles are here to stay and are no fad unless they are carelessly and unjustly treated as such.

QUALITY-CIRCLE STYLES: AMERICAN VERSUS JAPANESE

The assertion that QCs are here to stay if implemented properly is based on the American interpretation of circles rather than the already-entrenched Japanese variety. The authors feel that the two are clearly different in nature and would like to clarify this difference as well as predict the path that the Americanization of QCs is likely to take. The basic difference, summarized in Figure 1, is a reflection of deep, cultural dissimilarities. The intention of this discussion is not to pass judgment on either culture, but to describe the distinctions as they exist and their implications for QC implementation. This is not to say that the quality circle will necessarily flourish with American alterations; some characteristics or conditions must be changed if we are to realize success with this innovative tool.

American Emphasis	Japanese Emphasis
Individualism	Collectivism
Competition	Collaboration
Focus on company profits and growth	Focus on human competence
"Minimization" decision making	"Maximization" decision making
High reliance on status lines	Low reliance on status lines

Figure 1. Cultural Differences Between the United States and Japan

Individualism Versus Collectivism

The most obvious distinction lies in the respective self-images of the people themselves. Japan is a group-oriented society, and its inhabitants spend much of their lives working in cooperation with others. This cooperative behavior occurs in the family, which is still an extended one primarily; in public, where group-bathing facilities are common; and in the context of the work organization, where decisions are the responsibility of some-times-large teams of individuals.

Americans, on the other hand, have a heritage of individualism. Our families are nuclear; on the streets and in public places such as bars or restaurants, we congregate in twos and threes, usually no more; at work decisions are often made by key executives working alone. The 1980 U.S. Census indicated that nearly one quarter of all Americans live alone, a situation almost unheard of in Japan. This emphasis on individuality is closely tied to our tradition of competition and is certain to affect our implementation of QCs.

Competition Versus Collaboration

Although competition is far from nonexistent in Japan, America is the embodiment of the "all-or-nothing" variety. As is evident in the fierce combat of many of our sports and our television dramas, we tend to see things as right or wrong, win or lose, good or evil.

The Japanese are much more likely to think in terms of how to work together for the best results. When one person wins, so does everyone else. This attitude is facilitative for the work of quality circles, but the lack of it will certainly not eliminate American organizations as potential QC users. Quality circles in our country will find a way to make the best use of the competitive spirit that so extensively pervades our culture.

Company Profits and Growth Versus Human Competence

It is a long-recognized fact that American business people express a strong concern for the "bottom line." Because costs and profits are paramount concerns of most of our organizational managers, it is difficult for us to grasp the primary focus that the Japanese place on the human element. The goals of the Japanese are less measurable factors that take precedence over dollars earned: lifetime employment; loyalty; personal development; maximum utilization of human brainpower at every level; and satisfaction of human needs that are social, psychological, and even emotional in nature.

This emphasis on the human element probably accounts for the lack of statistical data that could demonstrate the bottom-line impact of quality circles on the Japanese economy. However, because Americans demand measurability of impact, our QCs will incorporate mechanisms for compiling numbers. This factor of measurability will certainly be an asset in demonstrating the value of quality circles to skeptics.

"Minimization" Versus "Maximization" in Decision Making

Another element that will influence the style of circles that evolves in the United States is the time required for making a decision, which represents a further source of difference between Japanese and American organizations. Many an American business person has suffered the frustration of waiting in a Tokyo hotel for what he or she considers a simple, "go-ahead" decision for a project or the purchase of a particular product. The Japanese take a great deal of time to consider all aspects of a situation and then even more time to achieve consensus among the individuals on whom the decision will have an impact.

In the American work place, in contrast, managers are praised for their skill at making quick decisions. Arriving at a consensus is an unfamiliar process; the closest facsimile is democratic voting for a majority rule. This style can work well in a QC provided that enough time is allowed for careful deliberation of the problem and the alternative solutions. American workers can, of course, learn the consensual decision-making process, but it will take time.

High Reliance on Status Lines Versus Low Reliance on Status Lines

The last difference covered in Figure 1 has to do with role perceptions, especially with regard to subordination. Although in Japan one's "place" is well known, there is less emphasis than in America on who is a supervisor and who is a subordinate. The important point is that each person is deemed an expert in the work that he or she does, whether it be supervision or production. Tapping that expertise for the best answers for the organization is the primary focus. In contrast, Americans have built fairly rigid lines of authority in organizations. We have supervisors and subordinates, "staff" and "line," labor and management, and countless other terminologies to keep our organizational relationships clear.

Because of this class-system heritage, the American quality circle, at least in its beginning stages, will be run in a rather tightfisted manner, with the supervisor playing the role of "the person in charge." This situation will change, however, as circle leaders begin to see the benefits of developing leadership in all members.

A PHILOSOPHICAL FOUNDATION
FOR QUALITY CIRCLES

If quality circles are to thrive in the United States, user organizations must adopt certain philosophical beliefs. The basic premise behind these beliefs is that every organization is a virtual gold mine of talent, brains, abilities, and ideas. When managers discover this valuable resource, the first step is taken toward a business philosophy conducive to quality circles.

Before defining the necessary elements of that philosophy, it is helpful to review the Statement of Purpose written by the Japanese Union of Scientists and Engineers (JUSE) to guide the development of QCs in Japanese organizations. This statement, which is made available to every participant in the Japanese QC system, notes the following critical goals of a quality circle:

- To contribute to the development and growth of the company;
- To respect the individuality of each member and to create a congenial setting in which work is meaningful; and
- To actualize the unlimited potential of human beings.

Foreign business people who read these elegant goals often wonder whether productivity, profits, product quality, sales, or cost reductions are even considered. They are, but only as by-products of reaching the "people goals," which are the raison d'etre of quality circles and which provide wonderful guidelines for Americans in determining their own philosophies on which to build QC programs.

The authors believe the key precepts of a QC organization to be the following:

- A firm expectation that people will take both pride and interest in their work if they experience autonomy and control over the decisions that affect them;
- An unwavering recognition of the dignity, humanity, and capability of every individual;
- A belief that each employee desires to participate in making the organization a better place in which to work;
- A requirement that any program in which the organization becomes involved must incorporate the development of human resources;

- A willingness to allow people to volunteer their time and effort for any company program;
- A commitment to the value of human creativity and to the phenomenon of synergy that results from creative contribution to the group; and
- An orientation toward wholism or the importance of each and every member's role and function in meeting organizational goals.

THE CIRCLE MOTIVATIONAL BASIS

Documented research indicates that QCs do, indeed, accomplish much of what they set out to do. The authors' observation is that they are tremendously popular with employees, so much so that several organizations maintain a QC "waiting list" of those who hope to obtain positions with existing circles. In addition, some companies have experienced positive side effects that have nothing to do with the actual activities or projects of the circles. For instance, there are often decreases in absenteeism and turnover, improved labor-management relations, and even better safety records. Determining the reason for these outcomes is important when contemplating the feasibility of a QC installation.

The authors believe that the potent but often unrecognized motivational groundwork on which QCs are built underlies their effectiveness. Motivation is defined as that which causes behavior. For many years behavioral scientists have proposed theories and techniques to be used by managers to increase employee satisfaction and production. A review of these theories and the ways in which they relate to quality circles may help to explain the success of QCs.

Taylor (1911)

More in the realm of management technique than pure motivation were the ideas of the "father of scientific management," Frederick W. Taylor. His approach, known as Taylorism, has been with us since the turn of the century and is based on his efforts in the steel industry in trying to determine the "one best way" of doing a job.

Taylor viewed the worker as a pair of hands to do the job; he did not recognize the thinking ability of the common laborer. Essentially he felt that high productivity was the result of the application of proper methods and not of some esoteric technique for satisfying human needs.

Although Taylorism is a far cry from the beliefs of most contemporary behaviorists, it was a major contributor to the concept of the quality circle.

Some ninety years after Taylor popularized statistical analysis of work, his methods have been adopted by circles with one major difference: Today it is the worker rather than the manager who uses the tools that he advocated.

Mayo (1945)

Practically every student of management has heard of the Hawthorne Studies, which were the work of Elton Mayo in a Western Electric plant located near Chicago in the Twenties and Thirties. After years of experimenting and compiling data obtained in more than 20,000 interviews with subject employees, Mayo and his team of researchers drew several conclusions that ultimately had a tremendous impact on the way in which organizations were managed.

The first tenet he proposed is commonly known as the Hawthorne Effect, which states simply that special attention to a group of workers will result in a positive improvement in behavior, even if the attention is of itself negative. A second conclusion was that social and psychological needs can be as motivationally effective as money or job security. Mayo also discovered that workers tend to congregate in informal groups and that these seemingly unimportant associations have the power to set and enforce production standards regardless of the standards set by the supervisor.

These ideas are critical to management if higher levels of production are to be achieved. The approach that makes sense and that works best is not to disband these groups but to tap their potential. Mayo enjoyed his greatest success when he formed work groups for the purpose of gathering their input for scheduling and other matters that affected their daily work life. Obviously, this is one of the basic principles of participative management and of QCs as well. Quality circles offer a structured opportunity for the organization to utilize the power of the informal group. In the process of solving work-related problems, workers are meeting their social and psychological needs. This is perhaps why attendance at circle meetings is normally high.

Maslow (1968)

Abraham Maslow's Hierarchy of Needs was an important expansion of the ideas that Mayo contributed to the growing theory of worker motivation. According to Maslow, every human being has six basic types of needs. The pyramidal shape shown in Figure 2 illustrates the hierarchical structure of these types, which are arranged in a sequential fashion from lower-order to higher-order needs. Maslow believed that when one level was satisfied, the

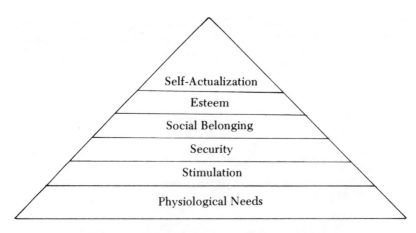

Figure 2. Maslow's Hierarchy of Human Needs[1]

---

individual immediately moved to the next level in the series without pause; all needs were pursued toward the ends of mental health and happiness. Thus, the hierarchy was initially portrayed as something that all of us climb up, and sometimes down, throughout our lives.

Over the years the interpretation of the hierarchy has become less rigid. It has been recognized that everyone approaches each level with a unique intensity, whether high or low. Now it is also believed that we do not necessarily move in sequence through the levels, but that we fulfill the various types of needs in the order in which they surface in our daily lives (Figure 3).

This concept is carried still further in Figure 4, which draws on Buckminster Fuller's design for the geodesic dome to depict a quality circle. The basic concept behind such a dome is that a geodesic structure covers the greatest amount of territory with the least amount of material and the greatest amount of strength of any design ever created. The basic concept behind group functioning is that each member has the same basic set of human needs and that healthy groups consist of individuals who help each other to meet these needs. If we combine these two concepts, we can assume that a healthy group can cover a greater amount of territory (projects) with a smaller amount of material (effort) and a greater amount of strength (effective solutions and ideas) than can anyone working alone.

---

[1]Adapted from A.H. Maslow, *Toward a Psychology of Being* (2nd ed.), Van Nostrand Reinhold, 1968. Used with permission.

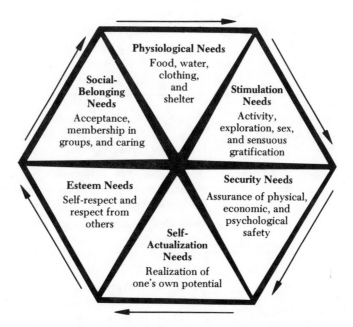

Figure 3. The Continual Cycle of Life Needs

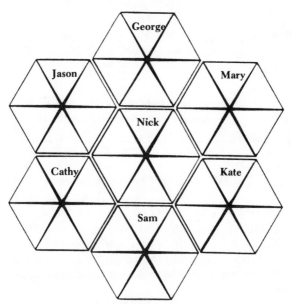

**Figure 4. Geodesic Group Structure
of a Quality Circle**

Thus, as clarified in Figure 5, a healthy group such as a quality circle is an important vehicle through which some of all but the most elementary needs can be gratified.

Type of Need (Maslow)	Ways in Which the Need Can Be Gratified Through QC Activity
Stimulation	Quality circles provide important ways to stimulate thought and reduce boredom in the work place.
Security	Through QCs employees can demonstrate their value to the organization and improve productivity, thereby making important and necessary contributions to their jobs.
Social belonging	Quality circles provide an accepted social structure; team building and acceptance are part of QC training.
Esteem	Successful QC projects receive recognition and generate respect for the talent and expertise of individual members as well as the team.
Self-actualization	Quality circles combine opportunities to use knowledge, judgment, and creativity with the freedom to decide how to contribute.

**Figure 5. The Role of Quality Circles
in Gratifying Individual Needs**

Argyris (1957)

Chris Argyris developed his Theory of Personality and Organization as a result of studying the development of the human organism from a dependent child to a fully functioning and responsible adult. His term "wholesale frustration" describes the conflict that arises when an adult is confronted with the rules, regulations, and restrictions typically found in the industrial organization.

For the past few decades in American organizational life, the need for individual freedom has been pitted against the need for the company to assert controls. In order to maintain control, organizations have often encouraged passive, childlike behavior, an approach that Argyris has deemed counterproductive in view of the fact that healthy adults need activity, independence, diversity, worthy challenge, autonomy, a sense of self-control, and equal status.

Quality circles encourage the development of adult behavior, even though such behavior may be threatening to managers who still believe in the "carrot-on-a-stick" tactic. Through training, voluntary participation, project selection and completion, and presentations to management, the organization can support the circle member in his or her natural development as a mature adult.

Likert (1961)

Rensis Likert, like Argyris, has identified inherent conflict between strict divisions of labor and cooperative, efficient, adult behavior. Consequently, he has stressed the need for a corporate-wide culture of cooperation and collaboration, which he has labeled "System 4." Organizations that are representative of "System 3" have some of the features of cooperation, but the stimulus for thinking and the final decisions come from management; these organizations are known as "consultative" because managers usually consult with employees before taking action.

"System-2" companies are benevolent but authoritative. Although decisions are made with the good of the employees in mind, they are made solely by those in the upper echelons, primarily because the rank and file are not seen as capable or competent in important decision making.

Finally, "System-1" organizations operate by imposing authority in a harsh manner or atmosphere for the purpose of exploiting the work force for all that can be gained. Little thought or consideration is given to the needs of the individual worker. These exploitative organizations are rare in today's work world.

Obviously, QCs are a form of System 4 when conditions are such that the circle members are free to choose their own projects and management is committed to a high level of acceptance of circle recommendations. In the authors' experience, some QC programs exhibit System-3 characteristics; projects are assigned to the circles, and management tends to be critical of the resulting suggestions. These forms have worked, but not as well as the System-4 types.

McClelland (1976)

David McClelland, a Harvard professor, has studied the goals of human behavior for many years. With a view that differs somewhat from that of Maslow, McClelland has theorized that humans pursue three basic objectives: power, achievement, and affiliation. Furthermore, he has asserted that although all of us seek these three, we do so in varying degrees.

In brief, a person with a high *power* orientation does not necessarily wish to dominate others, but does require a sense of control over events; he or she enjoys the challenge of an argument and plays to win. A person who has a high *achievement* orientation prefers to solve problems, overcome obstacles, and achieve challenging goals. Finally, the individual with a high drive for *affiliation* puts relationships with others above and beyond any other value in life; he or she avoids conflict and makes sure that things go smoothly in the personal realm. Thus, the relative intensity of these drives for an individual determines his or her personality.

Quality circles offer opportunities to satisfy each of these basic drives: the opportunity for autonomous action and self-control, which attracts those with high power needs; the chance to solve problems and receive recognition for a job well done, which satisfies those who are particularly achievement oriented; and the opportunity to experience esprit de corps, which appeals to those who are primarily oriented toward affiliation.

Herzberg (1966)

A study of two hundred engineers and accountants led Frederick Herzberg to develop his Motivation/Hygiene Concept, a theory of motivation that relates to those previously discussed. Herzberg has identified two sets of job factors that have an effect on workers. *Hygiene* factors are those that must exist in order to avoid employee dissatisfaction. These relate to the areas of salary, job security, work conditions, company policy, and administrative practices. In and of themselves, they are not motivational in nature. *Motivational* factors, those that can cause increases in employee production, include conditions related to achievement, recognition, advancement, personal growth, and the work itself.

Quality circles do not deal with the hygiene factors. Issues such as salary, company policy, or job security are not normally within the realm of circle discussion. Some work conditions can be addressed, but not the company-wide variety that have the greatest impact on employees. However, with regard to the need for the motivational factors identified by Herzberg, QCs once again succeed in transforming theory to reality. When an employee participates in a circle, he or she experiences recognition through measurable achievement, an enhanced feeling about the work performed, and learning and personal growth that improve the chances of advancement. All of these experiences are powerful motivators.

McGregor (1960)

Douglas McGregor offered another two-factor theory that has to do with the effect of the supervisor's perception of subordinates on the behavior of those subordinates. This was a new twist in the history of motivation theory because it did not deal with a person's internal needs and desires.

McGregor used the terms "Theory X" and "Theory Y" to describe opposite managerial attitudes. The Theory-X supervisor holds a caustic, cynical view of workers in which trust is almost entirely lacking. On the other end of the spectrum is the Theory-Y supervisor, who is an optimist and believes strongly in the basic capability, honesty, and positive intentions of workers. Thus, McGregor's premise applies the concept of self-fulfilling prophecy to what happens at work. A supervisor's behavior is consistent with his or her attitudes, be they "X" or "Y" or somewhere between these two extremes, and subordinates tend to act in accordance with the supervisor's expectations as revealed in his or her behavior.

The business approach that McGregor advocated was the use of small working groups built on trust and cooperation, and quality circles belong in this category. They require a company's managers to re-evaluate their ideas regarding the nature of people, even though in some situations this process is slow and painful.

Implications for the Future

New studies and theories about what motivates an individual to higher levels of productivity and a greater concern for quality are continually appearing. The common direction today is toward a participative management style in which every worker in the entire organizational hierarchy takes an active role as a responsible member of the company's business team. This organization of the future will be structured around the small group, which will work collaboratively to solve problems and take advantage of opportunities to meet organizational goals. The skills, abilities, and brainpower of all members will be pooled and utilized in the pursuit of new levels of effectiveness.

The authors' conclusion is that QCs are the forerunners in this wave of the future. Quality circles, which are firmly grounded in the major concepts of motivational theory (Figure 6), will open the way for changes in the manner in which we conduct business.

Theory or Principle	Compatible QC Concepts
"Scientific Management" (*Taylor*)	Quality circles place an emphasis on statistical tools and work analysis.
"Hawthorne Effect" (*Mayo*)	Special attention is available to circles via presentations to management and communication of results.
"Hierarchy of Needs" (*Maslow*)	The structure and processes of QCs help employees to meet higher-order needs, particularly those dealing with social belonging, esteem, and self-actualization.
"Theory of Personality and Organization" (*Argyris*)	Mature, responsible behavior is the essence of circle membership.
"System 4" (*Likert*)	Quality circles are a tool for achieving a participative, group approach to management.
Power, achievement, and affiliation motives (*McClelland*)	Quality circles provide opportunities for satisfying all three motives through autonomy, accomplishment, and social interaction.
"Motivation/Hygiene Concept" (*Herzberg*)	Quality circles supply the motivational factors of growth and learning, recognition, achievement, the chance for advancement, and an improved perception of the work itself.
"Theory X" and "Theory Y" (*McGregor*)	The managerial attitude on which QCs are based consists of respect, trust, and belief in the capability of workers to solve problems, create ideas, and take responsibility for their own behavior.

**Figure 6. Motivational Theories and Their Compatibility
with Quality Circles**

ADVANTAGES AND DISADVANTAGES
OF QUALITY CIRCLES

The authors have identified ten critical disadvantages as well as ten important advantages that a company should consider before proceeding with a circle program. The *disadvantages* are discussed in the following paragraphs.

1. An initial decrease in overall productivity can be expected. As circle participants turn from their daily work to the tasks of organizing themselves and undergoing training, the hours contributed to these efforts are nonproductive. Even if no formal measurement tool exists, the decline in output becomes apparent.

2. A large initial investment of time and money is required for a concept that is essentially new and unproven. A number of factors must be considered, such as worker "down time" for training, meeting, and planning as well as the financial outlay required for a facilitator, professional training materials, consulting fees, and so forth. In the authors' experience, the initial expenses range from $40,000 to $75,000; sometimes companies spend more, but rarely do they spend less.

3. The chance of error increases initially. This happens whenever change is introduced into an organization. Mistakes are inevitable at first as employees adjust to a new way of doing things, and these errors can be magnified to cast a negative shadow on a QC program.

4. Some employees are excited and challenged by a change and expect big results from the program within a short time. Because such results rarely occur quickly, some disappointment arises and may even lead to a small dropout rate.

5. Quality circles may threaten traditional authority structures. This is because the QC concept is built on an unfamiliar idea, that of empowering people at the lower levels of an organization so that they can competently participate in making the decisions that have an impact on them and their work. Thus, threatened authorities are likely to resist or even sabotage the project.

6. Those who are not in positions of authority may feel threatened as well. Employees who have grown used to depending on their supervisors for direction and who have lost their initiative feel uncomfortable with QCs. Interestingly enough, the authors have found that these people are most commonly older workers and those very new to the company.

7. At the beginning of a circle program, it is probable that some time will have to be spent in developing trust and interpersonal security. This probability arises from the fact that American organizations share a long history of mistrust between supervisors and subordinates.

8. Quality circles are meant to be an integral part of organizational life. They are not a temporary project to be accomplished at a specific point in time. However, because Americans tend to see things in terms of beginnings and ends, some individuals experience difficulty in perceiving the temporal characteristics of QCs.

9. After circle implementation a period of confusion ensues. This is always the case as people experiment with new ideas, new skills, and new roles.

10. The work accomplished by QCs necessitates changes in the existing system of controls. Such an outcome is consistent with the purpose of circle members, which is to analyze the work they do; to identify problems, obstacles, or opportunities; and to improve their work by systematically developing alternatives.

All ten of these disadvantages could certainly be enough to deter an installation. However, when considered separately, each can be planned for so that its impact on the company and the program is diminished.

On the other hand, the *advantages* that are described in the following paragraphs can easily be maximized.

1. The increased emphasis on training and developing employees is beneficial to everyone. Skills and knowledge that are applicable in every phase and level of work are obtained in formal training and in practice in circle meetings.

2. Quality circles promote a high level of productivity and quality consciousness. This effect extends beyond the circles to those who are not members. A minimum increase of 10 percent in overall productivity has been attributed to QCs in user companies.

3. Not only is productivity enhanced, but the way in which it is measured is refined. Most sectors of the American economy have, at best, an unsophisticated method for measuring their output. The number of products produced or dollars generated is just one factor that affects productivity; many other elements should be considered, and QCs spend a great deal of time determining these elements and ways to control them.

4. Circle members take an active role in keeping expenses down. Often QCs present employees with their first opportunity to appreciate the rationale behind cost-reduction efforts and to contribute to these efforts.

5. Participating employees experience increased motivation and pride in their work. These beneficial and interrelated side effects of QCs result from the employees' new opportunity to add their own ideas to their jobs. The satisfaction of helping to meet the challenges offered in the work place eventually translates into higher quality and craftsmanship.

6. Destructive competition, infighting, rivalry, and politics diminish. Circle members not only learn and use the skills of problem solving; they also learn new ways of working together toward common goals. A new collaborative spirit germinates and grows throughout the organization.

7. Those in positions of authority, whether they participate in circles

or not, benefit from the new management style that accompanies QCs. The gradual movement toward inclusion and participation offers every supervisor the experience of new management techniques and a new role.

8. The organization's entire system of planning is improved. Quality circles rely on the establishment of concrete, measurable, and specific goals as a part of short-range planning, and this future orientation permeates each department.

9. The organization is able to tap its store of brainpower and human potential. Even those who are cynical about employee thinking ability gradually see the proof of this ability in the results achieved by the circles.

10. Circle members receive recognition for their activities. Quality circles are highly visible entities; acknowledgment of their work is guaranteed if they are given the freedom to meet, to think, and to solve problems. Most modern managers agree that recognition is valuable as a positive motivator.

These disadvantages and advantages are not "set in cement." The way in which an organization designs and carries out its QC program and the care with which problems are handled determines the balance between the advantages and the disadvantages. The organization that proceeds with caution, practicality, and realism weighs the positive and negative factors before making a decision to implement. Completing the assessment form in Figure 7 according to the following instructions can be of help in making the necessary evaluation. This form is based on a list of the advantages and disadvantages just discussed.

1. Under "Advantages" two factors apply: "Likelihood of Occurrence" and "Relative Degree of Desirability." Using a scale of 1 to 5, where 1 is the lowest assessment and 5 is the highest, rate each of these factors for every advantage listed and write the appropriate numbers in the blanks provided. When both blanks have been filled for each item, multiply the two numbers in the blanks and list the result. When this process has been completed for all ten advantages, add the numbers in the column of results and write the total in the blank provided.

2. Under "Disadvantages" two factors also apply: "Likelihood of Occurrence" and "Relative Degree of Undesirability." Using the same scale of 1 to 5, rate each of these factors for every disadvantage listed and fill in the blanks accordingly. When both blanks have been filled for each disadvantage, multiply the two numbers in the blanks and list the result. When this has been done for all disadvantages, add the numbers in the column of results and write the total in the proper blank.

3. If the total for the disadvantages outweighs that for the advantages, consider canceling or postponing implementation.

	Likelihood of Occurrence	Relative Degree of Desirability
Advantages		
1. Increased emphasis on training and development	_____ x	_____ = _____
2. Increased productivity	_____ x	_____ = _____
3. Refined measurement of productivity	_____ x	_____ = _____
4. Consciousness of costs	_____ x	_____ = _____
5. Increased satisfaction and pride	_____ x	_____ = _____
6. Collaborative spirit	_____ x	_____ = _____
7. Practice of participative management style	_____ x	_____ = _____
8. Improved planning	_____ x	_____ = _____
9. Maximization of use of human resources	_____ x	_____ = _____
10. New vehicle for recognition	_____ x	_____ = _____

Total of Results for Advantages _____

	Likelihood of Occurrence	Relative Degree of Undesirability
Disadvantages		
1. Initial drop in productivity	_____ x	_____ = _____
2. Large initial investment	_____ x	_____ = _____
3. Increased chance of error at first	_____ x	_____ = _____
4. Disappointment because of unrealistic expectations	_____ x	_____ = _____
5. Threat to existing authority	_____ x	_____ = _____
6. Threat to employee status quo	_____ x	_____ = _____
7. Time loss due to efforts to correct mistrust in motives	_____ x	_____ = _____
8. Misunderstanding of the nature of QCs	_____ x	_____ = _____
9. Initial confusion	_____ x	_____ = _____
10. Threat to existing controls	_____ x	_____ = _____

Total of Results for Disadvantages _____

Figure 7. Advantages and Disadvantages Assessment Form

BUDGETARY CONSIDERATIONS

As is the case with many programs that permeate the organization and are complex enough to involve intangibles, the budgeting of quality circles is a process in which careful scrutiny of each expenditure is necessary.

Much of the "bandwagon" movement toward QCs is the result of reported returns on investment of 20 to 1 or more. It is certainly true that quality circles are effective; when properly installed and expanded, they easily pay for their cost of operation and generally return the organization's initial investment within a maximum of two years. However, a return of 20 to 1 is an exaggeration; the authors' supposition is that every direct and indirect cost has not been included in such estimates. A more logical ratio that can be expected is 2 or 3 to 1 in two years.

A quality-circle budget consists of two parts, a pilot program and an expansion plan, both of which involve direct and indirect costs. Thus, the total of all four types of costs is the amount that should be sought and communicated to senior management and to the organizational members when the program is publicized. *Direct* costs are those incurred directly as a result of the program or those immediately attributable to the program. Examples are expenditures for training materials, a full-time facilitator's salary, and printing of manuals and guides. *Indirect* costs, in contrast, are those that the company incurs regardless of the QC program, but that represent the program's actual use of the company's assets. Included in this category are expenditures for senior-management time, employee time, planning time, and meeting space.

Budgeting for a Pilot Program

Figure 8 is an example of a pilot-program budget prepared for a company of 2,500 employees in a large, midwestern city. The following is an item-by-item explanation of the types of *direct costs* covered in this figure.

1. *Facilitator's Salary.* A full-time QC facilitator is paid from $12,000 to $30,000 per year, depending on the specific duties of the position, the individual's training, and the company's location.

2. *Benefits.* One-third of the salary is the normal rate for a fringe-benefit package.

3. *Training Materials.* Such "materials" include a leadership-training session and at least eight QC training sessions; their cost varies if the training is developed in house.

4. *Printing.* This expenditure is the cost of reproducing all training materials.

Pilot-Program Budget (7/1/80 - 12/31/80)

Direct Costs

Facilitator's salary		$12,000
Facilitator's benefits		4,000
Training materials		7,000
Printing		3,000
Consulting fees		8,000
Office Supplies		1,000
Travel		800
Recognition program		2,000
	Subtotal	$37,800

Indirect Costs

Office space		$ 4,800
Equipment depreciation		800
Utilities, insurance, and so forth		2,500
Senior management's time		6,720
Implementation team's time		2,160
Employees' meeting time		
QC members		6,656
Leadership training		5,760
"Sales" to management		1,500
"Sales" to union		510
Clerical support		2,080
	Subtotal	$33,486
Total Cost		**$71,286**

Figure 8. Example of a Pilot-Program Budget

---

5. *Consulting Fees.* These fees are paid for outside assistance, when required, in designing the program, conducting the initial leadership training, and any external training of the facilitator.

6. *Office Supplies.* Internal and external communications and miscellaneous materials are included.

7. *Travel.* This category covers trips to observe QC programs in other companies as well as trips to external facilitator-training sessions.

8. *Recognition Program.* This cost reflects the amount set aside for recognizing the accomplishment of stated goals. In the sample case, a sum of $500 was allotted for each of four pilot circles.[2]

The explanation of the *indirect costs* listed in Figure 8 is as follows. Although the amounts that appear in the figure are specific to one particular organization, they provide a gauge of the expenses that can be expected in any pilot program.

1. *Office Space.* The expenditure for such space depends on local rates. In this case one hundred square feet, at a cost of $8 per square foot on a monthly basis, were used for the facilitator and circle meetings over a period of six months.

2. *Equipment Depreciation.* This category includes the dollar amounts allocable for the depreciation of office furniture, furniture for the meeting room, and equipment used in training for the pilot period. If new equipment or furniture is purchased for a program, this expenditure becomes a direct cost instead.

3. *Utilities, Insurance, and So Forth.* These expenses reflect the company's normal overhead charge. The amount is usually assessed per square foot of space used.

4. *Senior Management's Time.* Generally such time is spent attending the preliminary "sales" presentation, visiting QC meetings, serving on the steering committee, or participating in leadership training. The cost in this case was for eight senior managers, each with an average salary of $35 per hour, who spent four hours per month supporting the six-month pilot.

5. *Implementation Team's Time.* The members of this team design and plan the QC program and implement leader training. The sample organization paid six individuals, each at a rate of $15 per hour for twenty-four hours, to accomplish these tasks.

6. *Employees' Meeting Time.*

—QC Members. This cost pays the salaries of circle participants for the time that they spend in their meetings. The amount shown in the example, based on an average hourly rate of $8 per employee, paid for eight members per circle who met one hour per week for twenty-six weeks.

—Leadership Training. This expenditure pays the salaries of those chosen to be circle leaders while they are being trained for their positions. In the case cited in Figure 8, twenty supervisors and others, each averaging $12 per hour, participated in a three-day session.

---

[2]Although the company was advised to limit the pilot project to *three* circles—the number recommended by the authors as a maximum—the employees involved felt that sufficient resources existed to support four.

—"Sales" to Management. An informational presentation is necessary to "sell" the QC concept to management and to generate pilot volunteers. The company that conducted the sample pilot held a one-hour session attended by one hundred managers and supervisors, each averaging $15 per hour.

—"Sales" to Union. A similar presentation is often required to "sell" QCs to the union in question. The sample organization held a three-hour meeting attended by six managers, each averaging $15 per hour, and eight union officers, each of whom averaged $10 per hour.

7. *Clerical Support.* Some clerical work always arises from a pilot program. At a cost of $8 per hour in the sample case, ten hours of clerical support were used per week for twenty-six weeks.

Not all programs are budgeted in as much detail as the one used in the example. However, when developing a QC program, the implementation team would be well advised to overstate the costs somewhat and to demonstrate in the "sales" presentations that all possible expenses have been recognized and accounted for. Also, because some of the indirect costs would be incurred regardless of the program, management can cooperatively minimize their importance. Most senior managers are fully aware of these indirect costs, but appreciate acknowledgment of such expenses through their appearance in the budget.

Budgeting for Expansion

The expansion budget is identical in form to the pilot budget except that it omits start-up costs. Usually it is compiled on an annual basis. Figure 9 presents an example that is based on an expansion rate of two QCs per month. The amounts have been determined by using the same figures that were used in the pilot-budget example.

Most senior managers notice that the indirect costs comprise almost 64 percent of the total budget. As with the pilot-program budget, these costs would be incurred by the company regardless of the QC program; therefore, the real decision to be made is that of committing $52,600 to the effort.

Determining the Return on Investment

When dealing with a QC program that has not yet started, forecasting the rate of return on investment is a mostly subjective process. However, documentation from other user companies, such as that presented in Figure 9, can be helpful in adding some objectivity to such a forecast.

Expansion-Plan Budget (1/1/81 - 12/31/81)

Direct Costs

Facilitator's salary		$24,000
Facilitator's benefits		8,000
Printing		3,000
Office supplies		2,000
Travel		1,600
Recognition program		14,000
	Subtotal	$52,600

Indirect Costs

Office space		$9,600
Equipment depreciation		1,600
Utilities, insurance, and so forth		5,000
Senior management's time		13,440
QC members' time		46,592
Leadership training		11,520
Clerical support		4,160
	Subtotal	$91,912

Total Budget $144,512

Figure 9. Example of an Expansion-Plan Budget

The simplest way to approach this task is to use an average savings figure per circle in combination with the total-budget amount in Figure 9. For example, let us assume that each QC will return an average of $15,000 to the company through cost savings and productivity increases over a year's period. First we multiply $15,000 by 28, the number of pilot circles that served as the basis for Figure 8 plus the number added by the end of the first expansion year, and arrive at a projected savings of $420,000 for the second expansion year. We then divide the $420,000 by the total-budget amount in Figure 9, $144,512, which yields a projected return on investment of approximately 291 percent—a rather startling figure in view of the fact that costs have probably been overstated and savings understated.

Obviously, given this type of potential return, those responsible for planning a QC program can afford to be conservative in their estimates. Because managers typically think that a 20- to 30-percent return is excellent, there is no value in trying to understate costs or overstate savings.

A potential return of 291 percent will attract anyone's attention and will demonstrate the value of a QC program.

ASSESSING AN ORGANIZATION'S CHANCES FOR QUALITY-CIRCLE SUCCESS

The check list in Figure 10 presents various organizational requirements for a QC project; completing this check list can be useful in determining an organization's chances for project success. In addition, the instrument in Figure 11 is included for measuring an organization's receptivity to change based on three levels of operation: *maintenance, synergy,* and *environment.* The possibilities of successful QC implementation can be further assessed with this tool. The results obtained will be subjective but useful.

The section of the instrument entitled "Maintenance Level" is designed to specify the degree of managerial satisfaction with the way in which the organization is currently operating. The authors' premise is that an organization in difficulty, like an animal in pain, embraces change in an effort to find relief; the organization that is functioning satisfactorily is more likely to resist change efforts such as those involved with installing QCs.

The section entitled "Synergistic Level" measures the condition that exists when people have found ways to work in harmony. By contributing their ideas and abilities to a common pool, they achieve a greater result than can be expected from each individual working alone. It is the authors' experience that positive organizational attitudes and synergistic teamwork lead to change.

Finally, it is as important to look outside the company as it is to look inward. The section entitled "Environmental Level" is included for the purpose of measuring the amount of influence that external forces wield. An organization that exists in a relative vacuum finds few reasons to make changes; however, when government agencies, community groups, and industrial associations and unions exert an influence on the way in which a company is run, of necessity the ability to respond in a timely manner is developed.

A third evaluation form is presented in Figure 12, which deals with barrier identification. Measuring the organization's receptivity to change is important but incomplete without awareness of the specific barriers to be faced in QC implementation. Such awareness leads to a greater ability to deal with these obstacles and, consequently, to a greater chance for success. The authors believe that very few companies are totally incompatible with quality circles as long as careful preparation is made before installing them.

☐ The managers and supervisors involved have been determined to be skilled at teamwork.

☐ It has been verified that a general attitude of support for the program exists from the top down.

☐ The organization has ospoused a Theory-Y approach to people.

☐ Measurable productivity goals have been set for the program and the circles.

☐ A well-structured system for two-way communication has been set up.

☐ The participating managers and supervisors have been trained as intensively as circle members.

☐ A system has been developed for reporting results to management, and this system has been communicated to everyone involved.

☐ A facilitator has been hired or appointed to conduct leader training.

☐ It has been agreed that the circles are to have access to group-expense information for the application of cost-reduction and value-analysis techniques.

☐ Provision has been made for the circles to have access to in-house expertise.

☐ A system for formal recognition (and rewards, if desired) has been established.

☐ Adequate staffing and funding have been provided for the program.

☐ Specific and appropriate places have been determined for circle meetings.

☐ Space has been created within the work area for the display of physical evidence of circle activities.

☐ A realistic time frame for achieving results has been established.

☐ The organization has instituted a productivity measure.

Figure 10. Check List of Organizational Requirements for QC Success

☐   It has been acknowledged that the circles are to be given room to make mistakes.

☐   All of those involved have been given written guidelines and established policy for direction.

Figure 10 (continued).

Directions: Answer the following questions to the best of your knowledge and ability. Then follow the procedure for Interpretation of Results at the end of this instrument.

Maintenance Level

Within the past year:

Yes	*No*	
☐	☐	1. Have any top-level executives expressed dissatisfaction with the company's performance?
☐	☐	2. Have any top-level executives been shifted to new positions?
☐	☐	3. Has any area or problem been a constant source of worry or concern within the company?
☐	☐	4. Has the board of directors expressed any specific concerns to senior management?
☐	☐	5. Has the company performed at lower than the industry standard?
☐	☐	6. Have profit or growth targets fallen below management expectations?
☐	☐	7. Have attempts been made to unionize any segment of the work force?
☐	☐	8. Have there been any major setbacks or reversals in market share or product introduction?
☐	☐	9. Have any major new ideas or approaches been implemented in the work place?
☐	☐	10. Have there been any significant increases in turnover, scrap, or absenteeism rates?

Figure 11. Feasibility Assessment for QC Intervention

Yes   *No*

☐ ☐   11. Has any budget item risen significantly out of proportion to other budget items?

☐ ☐   12. Have any takeover attempts been made by another company?

☐ ☐   13. Have any new divisions been added?

☐ ☐   14. Have there been any major reorganizations?

☐ ☐   15. In your opinion do top executives have more to gain rather than lose by innovating within the company?

Synergistic Level

☐ ☐   1. Does the senior-management team ever participate in team-building sessions?

☐ ☐   2. Are the company's managers frequently reminded to cooperate with each other?

☐ ☐   3. Is any type of matrix system used within the company?

☐ ☐   4. Are enough conference rooms available for meetings?

☐ ☐   5. Do all of the top executives usually meet together rather than in one-on-one sessions?

☐ ☐   6. Is "empire-building" activity low, indicating defensiveness and the perception of powerlessness?

☐ ☐   7. Are most decisions that affect more than one area reached by consensus?

☐ ☐   8. Is management by objectives or outcomes used and supported?

☐ ☐   9. Do operating departments frequently ask for support from each other?

☐ ☐   10. Do the top executives present a united front when new or unusual decisions are announced?

Figure 11 (continued).

☐ ☐ 11. Is a rotational system of management ever used?

☐ ☐ 12. Are top managers and executives encouraged to take sabbatical leave?

☐ ☐ 13. Does the company have an organization-development function or department?

☐ ☐ 14. Does the company have a successful suggestion plan?

☐ ☐ 15. Is the president a good delegator?

Environmental Level

Yes   *No*

☐ ☐ 1. Is the company the only major employer in the area?

☐ ☐ 2. Is the company highly regulated by state or Federal agencies?

☐ ☐ 3. Does the company have a predominantly conservative corporate image?

☐ ☐ 4. Is the surrounding work population relatively stable?

☐ ☐ 5. Is the community a relatively no-growth or slow-growth area?

☐ ☐ 6. Do employees have to travel over fifty miles to attend a college or university?

☐ ☐ 7. Are other area businesses predominantly unionized?

☐ ☐ 8. Do the top executives have close political ties to state or Federal officials?

☐ ☐ 9. Is the company a frequent target for lawsuits and discrimination claims?

☐ ☐ 10. Are the company's customers or clients primarily located in a limited geographical area?

Figure 11 (continued).

Interpretation of Results

1. Add the following:

   • Number of *Yes* answers in the *Maintenance Level* _____

   • Number of *Yes* answers in the *Synergistic Level* _____

   • Number of *No* answers in the *Environmental Level* _____

   Total _____

2. The maximum possible total is 40. Compute the percentage of 40 represented by your total and list this percentage below.

   Percentage _____

3. Determine your estimated chances for introducing a successful QC intervention by locating your percentage on the following scale:

Percentage	Chances for Success
0 to 30	Negligible
30 to 50	Fair
50 to 70	Very good
75 to 100	Excellent

Figure 11 (continued).

The Company's History

☐ Past program failures (such as MBO, zero-based budgeting, and so forth) may be linked negatively to quality circles.

☐ The company has recently suffered a sharp financial downturn.

☐ Within the past five years, a union has been voted in.

☐ Within the past five years, a work stoppage, slowdown, or strike has occurred.

Figure 12. Check List for Barrier Identification

☐   An iron-willed company founder or chief executive officer still holds the controlling reins tightly.

The Company's Management

☐   Most managers have been around for a long time and are firmly entrenched in their positions.

☐   The "carrot-on-a-stick" tactic is the most popular approach to managing workers.

☐   There are many positions in which the holder has responsibility but no authority.

☐   Infighting, politics, and territoriality are prevalent among managers.

☐   Crisis management is the overriding policy of the company.

☐   Managers take care to avoid risks in their decision making.

☐   Problem solving begins with a WFII approach: Whose Fault Is It?

☐   Most jobs seem to result in a dead end; there is little or no emphasis on career or personal development, succession planning, or training.

Prevailing Employee Attitudes

☐   A union represents and is usually at odds with management.

☐   A union represents employees and is usually at odds with management.

☐   Employees are rapidly leaving the company and citing "better pay" with competitors as their incentive.

☐   Absenteeism is especially high on Mondays and Fridays.

☐   Grievances continue to be pressed, even though solutions appear obvious.

☐   Employees say that their objective is to put in their time, receive their paychecks, and nothing more.

Figure 12 (continued).

THE BASIC STRUCTURE OF QUALIT

Although some flexibility is appropriate in designing
particular organization, a basic framework should be
shows the ways in which a typical QC program mir
power structure of the organization. This imitative cnaracteristic is an
important factor in integrating circles into organizational life.

At the top of the QC hierarchy is the *steering committee,* whose
members include representatives of upper management, human-resource
and personnel people, and the company QC administrator. It is the
responsibility of this prestigious group to oversee the activities of the circles
and to provide them with the broad guidelines and policies needed to
coordinate their efforts. When large-scale projects are undertaken, it is
often this group that sits in review at the presentation to management.
Membership on the steering committee may be permanent or rotating in
nature, and the committee usually meets monthly.

Two special roles, QC administrator and QC facilitator, are also
identified in Figure 13. Depending on an organization's size and particular
needs, these roles may constitute separate positions, or they may be
combined into the same position. The authors have found that a very large

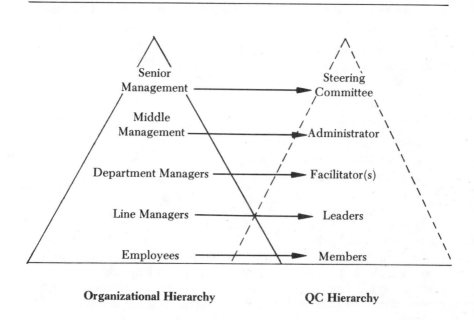

Organizational Hierarchy   QC Hierarchy

Figure 13. Interrelationship of Organizational and QC Structures

pany (more than 5,000 employees) generally needs one administrator nd many facilitators supporting various departments; an organization of medium size (800-5,000 employees) usually opts for a small staff of facilitators; and in small firms (fewer than 800 employees) one person acts as both facilitator and administrator of the program.

The QC *administrator* is the program's chief statistician, coach, and fan. Because a great deal is at stake in a program of this kind, the administrator must take care to establish and maintain detailed records and a reliable system of communication. Scheduling of training, presentations, and other related events is another important function of the administrator. The chief responsibility, however, is to support the company's facilitator(s) in any way possible. For example, the administrator is frequently called on to solve minor problems between departments, to listen to a discouraged facilitator who is having difficulty with a circle, to visit a QC to discuss the company-wide program, to talk to a nonparticipating department about QCs, or to compile information requested by the steering committee. The administrator is also the company's primary contact with outside people and companies that request information on the QC program.

It is possible to recruit the administrator from any of several sources. He or she may be a training specialist, a line manager, or someone from outside the company who has previous experience in QC administration. In any case this person may play an important role in any or all of the following activities:

- Designing and organizing the QC program;
- Training employees as circle members;
- "Selling" the concept and program to the internal audience;
- Coordinating efforts among department facilitators;
- Budgeting the program;
- Expanding the program;
- Compiling a history of QCs in the company;
- Serving as a resource to the facilitators; and
- Generating external publicity for the program.

The role of *facilitators* is also a crucial one; it consists of keeping the circles on track and enthusiastic. As with administrators, facilitators may be members of the organization's training staff, or they may be line managers who are interested enough to spend a great deal of time in training and preparation for their function. Facilitators are actively involved with the circles on a daily basis and, therefore, engage in most of the following activities:

- Serving as a resource to the circles under their responsibility by providing their own expertise in QC tools and techniques or by making sure that other expert sources in the company are available for consultation;
- Conducting much of the leadership training and assisting in the design of new training requested by the circles;
- Reporting circle progress, on request, to the steering committee and/or the administrator;
- Handling projects involving more than one circle;
- Assuring proper communication among circles;
- Helping circles to prepare presentations for management; and
- Maintaining budgets and keeping cost records for circles.

Of course, other duties can be added to this list. The facilitator is an extremely busy person with a job that is ever changing and rarely repetitive.

Circle *leaders* have a different, but just as critical, job in making the QC program a success. Every circle must have leadership, whether it is designated or not. Most, if not all, organizations that institute QC programs initially train supervisors to be leaders. Later, when experience has been developed, nonsupervisory personnel who are circle members may be asked to assume leadership. The leader's major activities include the following:

- Facilitating the circle's meetings to ensure that everyone has a say and consensus is achieved;
- Helping in the gathering of information;
- Training circle members in group process and the use of various tools and techniques;
- Acting as a sounding board for ideas and suggestions;
- Keeping meetings positive and on track;
- Helping the circle to set and achieve objectives;
- Presenting suggestions to the facilitator;
- Arranging the attendance of company experts and other guests at circle meetings as appropriate;
- Keeping the circle informed about the status of previously submitted suggestions;
- Developing and training alternate leaders; and
- Arranging and scheduling presentations to management.

The QC leader is more a nondirective facilitator than an authority figure. His or her role is to help the circle become self-sustaining, with or without the presence of designated leadership, and this cannot happen if the leader begins with the idea of being the exalted ruler in the group. Such an attitude results in a dependency relationship between him or her and the circle membership, thus diminishing the chances for autonomous, mature teamwork. If a supervisor who plans to serve as leader has developed authoritarian techniques, these methods must be put aside in favor of an egalitarian style.

Every circle must record its accomplishments, its failures, and its historical development. The responsibility for doing so lies with the *recorder*, whose activities include the following:

- Recording the minutes of all meetings;
- Keeping track of QC suggestions and ideas;
- Recording and posting the results of past suggestions and projects;
- Reading the minutes of the last meeting at the start of each new meeting; and
- Handling all circle correspondence.

The role of recorder is most successfully handled when a rotational system of selection is used.

Expert resources are those internal, and occasionally external, persons who are invited to attend circle meetings to share their experiences and to answer questions from their own areas of proficiency. Sometimes they are asked to train circle members or to contribute cost-reduction or quality-improvement ideas.

The most important level of the QC hierarchy consists of the circle *members,* without whom the program could not exist. Each has the following important responsibilities to fulfill:

- Attending all meetings possible;
- Offering suggestions and ideas to the circle in good faith;
- Participating actively in the group process;
- Being accountable for the overall team spirit of the circle;
- Helping to stimulate discussion and results;
- Attending training sessions with a receptive attitude; and
- Contributing to the circle's goal-setting process.

The circle members are truly the lifeblood of the program.

REFERENCES

Argyris, C. *Personality and organization.* New York: Harper & Row, 1957.

Herzberg, F. *Work and the nature of man.* Mountain View, CA: Anderson World, 1966.

Likert, R. *New patterns of management.* New York: McGraw-Hill, 1961.

Maslow, A.H. *Toward a psychology of being* (2nd ed.). New York: Van Nostrand Reinhold, 1968.

Mayo, E. *The human problems of an industrial civilization.* Boston: Harvard Business School Division of Research, 1945.

McClelland, D.C. *The achieving society.* New York: Halsted, 1976.

McGregor, D. *The human side of enterprise.* New York: McGraw-Hill, 1960.

Snyder, R. (Ed.). *Buckminster Fuller: An autobiographical monologue/scenario.* New York: St. Martin's Press, 1980.

Taylor, F.W. *The principles of scientific management.* New York: Harper & Row, 1911.

PART II

A MODEL
FOR INSTALLING
QUALITY CIRCLES

Step 1

Strategic Planning

OVERVIEW

Before formally beginning Step 1, it is important to understand the concept to be implemented. The QC planner who knows the facts and understands the subject organization inside and out can confidently confront the obstacles that are sure to be encountered.

This type of knowledge and understanding becomes the suprastructure of the long-range strategic plan to be designed for the installation and expansion of quality circles within the organization. Strategic planning all but guarantees that a QC program begins effectively, stays on track, and produces the highest possible return on investment in human satisfaction and profits for everyone involved.

Step 1 typically begins when someone in the organization hears about quality circles and is intrigued by them. Although such a person may be a decision maker in the organization's top level, this is not always the case; circle programs have stemmed from every conceivable company function. In any case this individual usually wants to study the concept more thoroughly. Thus, a decision is made either to contact a professional as an expert resource or to proceed on one's own to determine the feasibility of QCs for the company; consequently, either the expert or the organizational member becomes the company's QC planner.

The nonexpert who chooses to prepare himself or herself for this role starts by reading extensively on the subject. The authors recommend the starter list of readings in the Appendix. It is also a good idea to contact nearby organizations that may be in the process of implementing quality circles and to talk to anyone who might provide ideas or information. In addition, it is advisable to attend a seminar or workshop to learn and *practice the required skills; many such events are offered in all areas of the country. In short, it is essential to educate oneself thoroughly about QCs and to become an expert who knows or can find the answers to any of the myriad of questions that will surface while following the authors' model. The primary purpose is to understand the facts before committing to the program.*

Next the planner seeks out potential supporters within the organization who will help to spearhead the effort. The objective is to enlist the company's most innovative, well-spoken, and well-regarded individuals—those who can contribute positively to the effort and to the necessary power base. The impact of such a coalition is considerable. The usual pattern is to undergo a slow process of generating interest and enthusiasm in informal discussions until a team of approximately four to eight members (including the QC planner) is ready to schedule a strategic-planning session.

The strategic-planning session can last from two to five days, during which the QC concept is examined thoroughly for its feasibility in the organization. The major results of this session are the decision to proceed, a written implementation plan that features goals and objectives for a three- to five-year period, a step-by-step strategy to meet these goals and objectives, and the identification of roles and responsibilities for carrying out the plan.

Although this procedure may seem difficult and involved, the authors are convinced that the initial effort and investment are essential to the success of a QC project. The strategic plan is the most important component of the authors' model; it is the cornerstone on which the program is built, and it is the item that must be "sold" to all levels of the organization. Therefore, high quality is a must.

In Step 1 the implementation team furthers its knowledge of QCs, engages in a great deal of rational thinking, and eventually develops a specific plan of action. All subsequent steps depend on this plan for support. In summary, the objectives of Step 1 are as follows:

- *To develop "expertise" in quality circles in each member of the team;*
- *To conduct an investigation into the feasibility of QCs in the organization;*

- *To identify all possible obstacles to success and to plan around them;*
- *To identify power bases in the organization and to design a strategy for incorporating them into the QC support system; and*
- *To compose an action agenda that covers at least the first three years of QC operation.*

CONTENT

After the QC planner has recruited people to join in this venture and these team members have agreed to spend a few days together in a formal fact-finding and planning workshop, it is necessary to organize an agenda that will help the team to achieve its goals. The following questions are representative of the types of issues that should be included in the agenda.

- What are quality circles?
- What is their history?
- Why do they work?
- Are they related to organization development? If so, in what way?
- What other organizations are using them? Have these organizations experienced success?
- What is the time frame for installation?
- When will we see results?
- What kinds of results can we expect?
- What advantages and disadvantages must be considered?
- What will the program cost?
- What are the organizational requirements?
- What is the best structure for QCs?
- What roles are to be played? Who will be responsible for each role?
- How can we tie QCs to productivity?
- What should be the requirements for the pilot project?
- What arrangements should be made for rewards and recognition?
- Why should people want to participate?
- How should training be handled?
- What type of advanced training is necessary?
- Will QCs be established in areas in which the work performed is not directly related to the output of the company's product or service (for example, the personnel department)?

- Do circles have goals? If so, what are some examples?
- Do we need a QC charter?
- What is our present organizational situation? In what direction is the organization presently headed?
- How do QCs "fit" what the organization is doing?
- Who should be involved in this project?
- To whom must we "sell" the idea, and how should we "sell" it?
- How can we generate organizational commitment?
- Can we expect opposition from any source? If so, how is it to be handled?
- What are the implications for the union?
- What are our objectives in instituting quality circles?
- Should we seek help from a consultant, purchase a prepackaged QC program, or design and implement a program ourselves?
- How does expansion take place?

Many of these questions have to do with the acquisition and analysis of knowledge. The QC concept must be clarified, and the team members must develop a working knowledge of the installation process. Every effort must be made to ensure that a common understanding is achieved.

Other questions will arise, and the answers will not all be found in books and articles. Often such answers are determined by focusing internally and by exploring the unique personality of the organization that is to become "home" for the QC project. Thus, it is important to understand the climate of the work place—how it is generated and how it affects the work produced. It is also necessary to define the management philosophy that exists and to assess whether it will support or detract from the program. In addition, all potential sources of conflict and opposition should be identified. These activities are essential because it is impossible to achieve an objective for the future without knowing the present conditions.

A good way to begin is to consider the current management philosophy. All important decisions and actions are based on this philosophy, and it plays a leading role in determining the quality of interpersonal relations in the organization. Each member of the implementation team also has his or her own philosophy at the outset; sometimes the various philosophies are radically different from the one espoused by the organization. For this reason it is advisable to examine these views of people and behavior as an introduction to the planning session.

A useful model for examining management beliefs is McGregor's (1960) continuum of Theory-X and Theory-Y beliefs, which is summarized in Figure 14. The team members attending the session should identify their positions along the continuum and explain their beliefs. It should be explained that because the descriptions presented in the figure are associated with "pure" types of management philosophies, the continuum allows the members to take stock of the organization and themselves in terms of the many shades of belief that exist between the two extremes. The more congruent the individual philosophies, the more likely the team's success.

Agreeing on a philosophy, however, is not all that is required. Given the nature of the team's mission, the authors believe that the zone of agreement must be in the area of the continuum between the numbers 6 and 9. Quality circles are a tool of participative management, and participative management is a way of organizational life that champions the dignity and value of people and demonstrates interpersonal trust. Principles other than these are incompatible with the theoretical basis of QCs.

After the team members have defined their own views, they apply the same principles of categorization to the organization. Initially they either brainstorm possible meanings of recent managerial actions and decisions, or they try to determine what a particular policy or procedure might communicate to those it guides. For example, a standing rule that an employee must punch in and out on a time clock for breaks may easily be interpreted as an expression of mistrust; it may be inferred that management places a higher priority on the time spent on the job than on the results achieved. This type of thinking would rate a 2 or 3 on the continuum as a Theory-X indicator. Generally, the greater the emphasis that the company

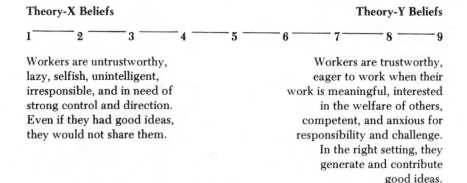

Figure 14. Continuum of Theory-X and Theory-Y Beliefs

places on profit versus people, authority versus autonomy, and exclusion versus participation, the more closely the company's management philosophy resembles a pure Theory-X type. If the team members agree that these characteristics apply, the strategic plan will not succeed readily unless it incorporates a significant degree of change.

One important piece of information uncovered by following the directions for self-analysis as well as organizational analysis of philosophy is the gap between the team members' general frame of reference and that of the company. The authors refer to this as the "congruency gap" (CG). For example, if the team appears to be operating from a philosophy of 8 on the continuum and the organization is determined to be functioning from a philosophy of 5, the applicable CG is 3. Any CG of 3 or above is considered to be significant and indicative of obstacles in the path that lies ahead.

A high CG is a warning flag that must be heeded. If the team members are significantly closer to Theory X than the company is, they should reassess their motives for considering QCs. If, however, the situation is reversed, as is more likely, this indicates potential conflict and riskiness in advocating an innovative project such as quality circles. Sizable CGs predict that meaningful results will take longer to realize, that the team's support-building effort will have to be more extensive, that more courage and patience will be required to deal with the inevitable frustration that will be experienced, that fewer sympathetic ears will listen to the team's suggestions, and that a broader and more comprehensive strategic plan that emphasizes measurable results will be necessary.

In the authors' experience, most CGs have been 3 or above, with the organization leaning toward Theory X. The very nature of doing business in the United States probably accounts for this development. For years, following a Theory-X line of thought and achieving the position of the top productive force in the world were concurrent happenings. In fact, it is possible that one might have caused the other. On the other hand, it is interesting to consider what might have been achieved if Theory-Y thinking had had a greater following. What is important is that the productivity needs of today, like quality circles, call for a viewpoint between 6 and 9 This is why the development of a strategy is so important when the organization has not yet arrived at this viewpoint.

Successful organizational interventionists make it their business to know and understand the systems of power, both formal and informal, that exist in the target organization. With an intervention such as quality circles, acquiring this knowledge is particularly important. Completing the following procedure will help the implementation team to visualize the power that exists and the ways in which it can support and/or detract from the team's efforts.

1. In Figure 15 write the names of up to twenty key people in the organization who might have an impact on the team's QC plans. These individuals might include members of senior management, influential middle or line managers, certain employees, and union officials.

2. Determine the relative formal power of each on a scale of 10, for which 0 represents *no* formal power (for example, a line worker) and 10 represents *absolute* formal power (for example, the chief executive officer). In each case write the appropriate number in the column entitled "Formal Power" in Figure 15.

3. Determine the informal power that each person might have with regard to the implementation and conduct of quality circles. A score for this type of power can range from -10, which identifies an extreme ability and inclination to detract from and sabotage the program, to +10, which identifies an extreme ability and inclination to be supportive of the effort. A score of 0 indicates a state of neutrality toward the program. (This second evaluation of key people will be more subjective than the first, but just as useful.) In each case write the appropriate number in the column entitled "Informal Power" in Figure 15.

4. Transfer the information from Figure 15 to Figure 16 by plotting the intersection of the two ratings for each person and writing that person's initials on the matrix at the point of intersection.

5. Refer to Figure 17 to interpret the results of the previous step. In general, the more initials that are placed in *quadrant IV*, the more confident the team can be of a program with a strong, positive power base; therefore, success can be well predicted.

If the majority of initials are placed in *quadrant III*, the team should proceed with a plan, but success should not be automatically assumed. It is necessary for the team to be flexible and prepared to deal with unforeseen situations as they arise.

When most initials are in *quadrant II*, the approach should be to plan small steps, take them one at a time, and analyze the situation after each. It may even be a good idea to rechart the organizational power after each step.

With a large number of initials in *quadrant I*, the team must do extremely careful, extensive planning. Quadrant I represents a very poor power base, which means that the team has a difficult task ahead of it.

It is essential to remember that the matrix is changeable when the proper strategies to rechannel power are implemented. All those who are potential problem sources should be identified, and change strategies should be developed to alter the ways in which they might use their informal power with regard to the program.

Name	Formal Power (0 to 10)	Informal Power (-10 to + 10)
1.		
2.		
3.		
4.		
5.		
6.		
7.		
8.		
9.		
10.		
11.		
12.		
13.		
14.		
15.		
16.		
17.		
18.		
19.		
20.		

Figure 15. Power Data Sheet

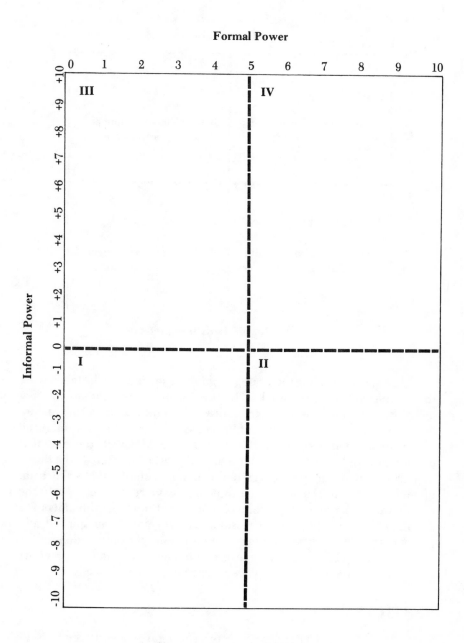

Figure 16. Power Matrix

Power Base

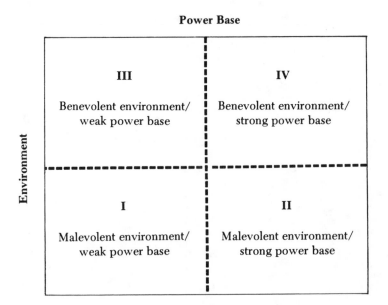

III Benevolent environment/ weak power base	**IV** Benevolent environment/ strong power base
I Malevolent environment/ weak power base	**II** Malevolent environment/ strong power base

Figure 17. Power-Matrix Interpretation

Ideas for completing the strategic-planning session may be taken from the sample agenda presented in Figure 18, in which most of the key questions previously discussed are addressed. Another noteworthy feature of this agenda is the distribution of presentation responsibilities among all of the team members. The QC planner, Lee Maxwell, decided that cooperation and synergy could be achieved most effectively in the three-day session if participation was built in. When she invited each team member to attend, she assigned a topic and gave references to help the member to research the topic. She also provided some helpful hints for a dynamic delivery. The resulting session was highly involving, spirited, and productive. Of course, a shared presentation is not the only option for the session. Other QC planners have presented and facilitated the entire meeting and have had similar success in accomplishing objectives.

PARTICIPANTS

It is possible for a QC planner to create a strategic plan and even to "sell" it on his or her own. However, as the quality circles eventually implemented will demonstrate, better ideas come from groups. The authors' experience indicates that the best results are obtained when a design team is used and the team members number no more than eight (including the QC planner).

Strategic-Planning Session for Quality Circles

Date: August 7, 8, and 9, 1979

Participants: Dale Shepard, Operations Manager
Chris Thompson, Production-Line Foreman
Lee Maxwell, QC Planner
Pat Arnold, Shop Steward
Terry Walker, Corporate Human-Resources Representative

Agenda

August 7

A.M.   Greetings and Introductions (L. Maxwell)
Why We Are Here (L. Maxwell)
Film: "If Japan Can . . . "
Quality Circles: Definition and History (L. Maxwell)
Report on Fact-Finding Mission (L. Maxwell)
How Quality Circles Function (D. Shepard)
Quality-Circle Structures (T. Walker)

Noon   Lunch

P.M.   Advantages and Disadvantages (P. Arnold)
Quality-Circle Goals and Charters (T. Walker)
Budgetary Considerations (T. Walker)
Time Frame for Installation (L. Maxwell)
Rewards and Recognition (T. Walker)
Decision: Should We Proceed? (C. Thompson)

August 8

A.M.   Quality-Circle Training (L. Maxwell)
Quality Circles and Indirect Labor (P. Arnold)
Force-Field Analysis of the Company (C. Thompson)

Noon   Lunch

P.M.   Continuation of Force-Field Analysis (C. Thompson)
Goal Setting for the Project (C. Thompson)
People-Power Charting (L. Maxwell)

Figure 18. Sample Agenda for a Strategic-Planning Session

August 9

A.M.   What Resources Are Available? (P. Arnold)

   Decision: Should We Design and Implement the Program Ourselves?
   (D. Shepard)

   The Strategic Plan (D. Shepard)

Noon   Lunch

P.M.   Continuation of the Strategic Plan (D. Shepard)

   Preparing for the "Sale" (C. Thompson)

   Assignments and Closure (C. Thompson)

Figure 18 (continued).

Also, as suggested previously, the most successful teams consist of those who are known to be innovators, who demonstrate enthusiasm for the QC concept, who have the ability to act collaboratively, and who can contribute to the power base to be built in preparation for Step 2—"selling" the concept to senior management.

Roles vary considerably within this team, but all members are considered to have equally useful contributions to make. Formal organizational status is not a primary consideration. More important is the collaborative, egalitarian character of the team, which will be echoed in the circles once they are integrated into the organization.

TIME FRAME

From the moment that quality circles are conceived of as a possibility until the implementation team begins its work, at least six weeks will have passed. This interim period should be filled with preparatory activity, such as planting the seeds of interest in the minds of potential supporters and team members, self-education and information gathering, planning the session, and visiting other organizations that use quality circles.

The session itself should last a minimum of two days and as many as five. Once it has been determined how much time must be spent in planning, it becomes necessary to decide how this time will be scheduled. A team within one of the authors' client organizations met twice a week for several weeks, and each of these one-hour sessions combined work with breakfast. Another team met in a comfortable, off-site setting for two twelve-hour planning days. A third simply scheduled three work days in the company conference room. The best arrangement is the one that most effectively meets the needs of the organization in question. After the conclusion of the planning session, no less time than two months will pass until the first meeting of the first pilot QC.

TIPS FOR SUCCESS

The QC planner should give careful consideration to this potpourri of recommendations; following these guidelines may make the difference between moderate and stunning success in a QC project.

- Choose implementation-team members who can be trusted to be fair in their consideration of the concept.
- Choose team members with differing perspectives of the organization and the project. Various points of view vitalize the planning session.
- Find and communicate a specific reason for each individual supporter to join the team.
- Do not oversell quality circles. Heavy-handed efforts to convert others will alienate them.
- Develop a check list of questions to be answered during the planning session.
- Write a team philosophy of management on which to base the plan.
- As a part of the plan package, develop a company charter that clearly defines structure, purpose, and philosophy.
- Identify every conceivable cost of the project.
- Chart the power of the organization and plan strategies to draw on the resources of supporters and to win over opponents.
- Plan to involve senior managers in the effort, especially as steering-committee members.
- Address the issue of sharing the profits reaped through quality circles.
- Integrate a communication vehicle into the design.
- Include in the plan an option of redecision for quality circles after a six-month trial period.
- Do not rush the project. Be patient and allow things to evolve.

REFERENCE

McGregor, D. *The human side of enterprise.* New York: McGraw-Hill, 1960.

"Selling" Quality Circles to Senior Management

OVERVIEW

Even though quality-circle projects have achieved impressive levels of success when initiated as grass-roots movements, that success can be multiplied when those at the top are actively involved in the organization's QC system. Unless the program is initiated at a high level in the organization, senior-management interest and involvement must be catalyzed and carefully nurtured.

One of the primary tasks of the strategic-design team is to determine how to generate this crucial commitment. Thus, the agenda for the planning session must incorporate time to develop a "sales plan" for Step 2. Those who are able to sell effectively attribute their success to the following sales techniques:

- Honesty—*being absolutely truthful about everything, including every cost and every disadvantage as well as advantage;*
- Personal appeal—*knowing the "target" well enough to address his or her personal motive for buying the product;*
- Brevity—*executing a clear and concise presentation of the facts and then closing quickly;*
- Expertise—*knowing the product well enough to handle any question and, in particular, any objection that might be raised; and*
- Preparation—*being 100 percent ready and rehearsed.*

Generally Step 2 is taken in a short meeting to which the members of senior management who are essential to the QC project are invited. For several weeks prior to this meeting, the implementation-team members will have been carrying out their assignments in preparation for one or more parts of the "sale." These parts will have been carefully orchestrated with a single goal in mind: to leave this important session with enthusiastically granted permission to proceed and the commitment of everyone in attendance to play an active role in the implementation and growth of the QC program.

The ways in which senior managers are involved depend on the unique characteristics of the organization, the particular senior managers who are addressed, and the strategic plan that has been developed. It is important that senior managers know what quality circles are and be willing to provide financial as well as verbal support.

The strength of the QC program is largely dependent on the strength of the foundation laid. The program can have no greater support than that received from senior management, and the purpose of Step 2 is to gain that invaluable backing. Of course, if permission to proceed has already been obtained along with an agreement to participate in strategic planning, this step can be eliminated.

CONTENT

The meeting with senior management is the end product of a long process of data gathering, informal support building, and careful design. The objective is to cover a great deal of material in a professional manner and in the shortest time possible. Much of the information found in Part I of this book will be helpful in the preparation for this meeting.

Most, if not all, of the following topics should be covered in the presentation:

- A definition of quality circles;
- A short history of QCs;
- Other organizations involved in QCs;
- How the present project came to be;
- The purpose of the meeting;
- Advantages and disadvantages of quality circles;
- Budgetary considerations and the projected return on investment;

- The strategic plan;
- Identification of company support;
- Request for support; and
- Questions and answers.

If the intention is to cover all of these matters in an hour, an average of five minutes can be allotted for each topic. This time limit can be achieved if the team members agree to a one-way presentation to the audience, which involves asking the senior managers to make notes of questions or concerns and to raise them in the final minutes allowed for discussion.

To maximize the potential for achieving the goal of this meeting, every tool available should be used. Clear, legible charts and graphs placed at eye level on an easel are quite effective. The use of an overhead projector and professionally prepared transparencies is also invaluable. If time allows, it is a good idea to show the NBC "White Paper" that was largely responsible for generating interest in the QC movement in the United States in 1981. This film, entitled "If Japan Can . . . ," is available for rent or purchase,[3] but it is advisable to ask around before spending money for the film because most companies that own it seem quite willing to lend it for no charge.

A detailed explanation of the previously suggested list of topics is as follows:

1. *A Definition of Quality Circles.* One or two sentences should suffice. The authors' suggestion is the following: *Quality circles are small groups of co-workers who meet regularly to statistically analyze and solve problems involving the work they perform.* Details of the definition will become clear as the presentation proceeds. This statement or one of the team's choosing can be put on a transparency with the key words underscored.

2. *A Short History of QCs.* Detailing every event in the evolution of quality circles is unnecessary. Instead, the best approach is to note the milestones, emphasizing the importation of the concept to the United States.

3. *Other Organizations Involved in QCs.* Citing approximately a half-dozen major companies that are using quality circles can work wonders in sparking interest. If they are local firms, so much the better.

---

[3]For information on obtaining this film, write to NBC, 30 Rockefeller Plaza, New York, NY 10020. Refer to it as *the 1981 NBC "White Paper" entitled "If Japan Can . . . ," narrated by Lloyd Dobbins.*

4. *How the Present Project Came to Be.* All team members should be introduced, and then the audience should be told how the QC planner became interested in a QC program for the company and how others were brought into the planning work. The senior managers should be given an overview of the activities in which the team has been involved in the past several weeks. This overview serves as an agenda for the remainder of the meeting.

5. *The Purpose of the Meeting.* It should be announced in a straightforward manner that the meeting has been called to enlist the full support of senior management in implementing a QC program in the company. It should also be stated that a rationale will be offered as the meeting progresses.

6. *Advantages and Disadvantages of Quality Circles.* Although it is tempting to downplay the disadvantages of QCs, this approach is not advised. Few senior managers are gullible enough to believe that advantages are not accompanied by disadvantages. When the benefits of the program are overplayed, those making the presentation appear to be dishonest; however, when both the advantages and the disadvantages are explained in such a way that they can be logically weighed, the presenters' credibility is enhanced along with their chance of "making the sale."

7. *Budgetary Considerations and the Projected Return on Investment.* This topic also requires the presenters to "tell all." For example, one implementation team with which the authors were familiar had initiated QCs and was fond of announcing a 20-to-1 return on investment (ROI) for its efforts. A careful look at these figures indicated that a return of 20 to 1 was accurate only if certain expenditures were excluded, such as wages for time spent in circle meetings, the full-time facilitator's salary, and assorted materials and supplies used in circle work. In fact, all that was really considered in this instance was the consultant's fee and the packaged training materials. The ROI was later calculated to be only 6 to 1 when these other legitimate costs were figured. Certainly a 600 percent return is very healthy and nothing to be ashamed of.

Because a correctly implemented QC program is always an advantageous investment, every possible cost should be included to determine a *minimum* rather than optimum ROI. At the end of the second or third year of QC operation, the team will feel much better about claiming the achievement of more than expected rather than less.

The authors suggest that a five-year projected ROI be determined and presented. Although forecasting this far into the future is difficult, it shows the audience that the team has thoroughly considered all possible types of expenses.

8. *The Strategic Plan*. During this part of the meeting, a summary of the product of Step 1 is presented. A milestone chart prepared as a handout serves well for this purpose when prefaced with the rationale for the plan. Major objectives should be highlighted in terms of the number of circles, improved productivity and product quality, and the ROI. It is critical that the plan be logical and include provisions for "selling" the program to middle and line management as well as the union, selecting pilot circles and establishing their structure, training, beginning circles, evaluating and refining the program, and expanding the program.

9. *Identification of Company Support*. Prior to this meeting, the team members will have been talking to people with influence throughout the organization, subtly generating the interest of select individuals without engaging in a "hard sell" for commitment. During this process the members will have identified key areas of support and, perhaps, one or more target areas for the pilot study. At this point in the meeting with the senior managers, the sources of support as well as resistance should be named and any ideas regarding possible placement of pilot circles should be mentioned. Such information further convinces the audience that the team is prepared for any obstacles that may arise.

A helpful way to keep track of both support and obstacles is to chart the power within the company (see Step 1). It is important to remember, however, that the specific results of power charting are for the use of the team and should not be presented in the "sale" to senior management.

10. *Request for Support*. This is the crux of Step 2. What has been covered in the meeting should be summarized briefly, and then the team's request should be stated in a manner similar to the following: "In order to proceed further with our plan, we need [time] , [space] , [people] , and [dollars] . Above all, we need your concurrence and your willingness to demonstrate your support by being involved in this quality-circle program." Instead of waiting for an answer, it is advisable to lead directly into the discussion that concludes the meeting.

11. *Questions and Answers*. Immediately after the request for support, the audience should be asked the following question: "Is there anything that you would like to know or ask about what is being proposed?" At this point the team members' knowledge and expertise are most important because the one-way presentation becomes a dialogue. The team should be prepared to answer any question and should be aware that objections will, indeed, be raised. As salespeople know, people habitually use such objections to gather more information and to avoid hasty decisions. Objections do not indicate nonacceptance, even though they may sound as if they do. When responding to these comments, it is wise to use *reflective-*

listening skills by repeating the speaker's objection to make sure that it is clearly understood. Then all of the facts should be presented, regardless of whether they affirm or negate the objection. Figure 19 presents six of the most common objections and responses to counter them.

Objection	Suggested Response
"America's culture is different from Japan's. Quality circles won't work here."	"Yes, our culture is different. However, American companies such as [examples] have been very successful in Americanizing QCs."
"It sounds as if we'd be giving a lot of power to the workers. Can we still keep them under control?"	"It's true that workers will have more control over the decisions that directly affect them. Your power won't change, though, because of the strong role you'll play in the steering committee and because you'll have the final say on ideas presented by the circles."
"You're going to form bargaining units? No way." (This objection is raised by those who fear unionization.)	"We're going to form 'thinking units' to work on productivity and quality. They will not deal with salary, work rules, or grievances. In fact, not one American company that uses quality circles has been unionized 'after installation.' "
"If circle members meet during work hours, productivity will decrease."	"At first you'll see a small decrease. But the circles will be learning to work 'smarter,' not harder. Our goal is a minimum increase in productivity of 10 percent at the end of the first year."
"How do we know that these meetings won't turn into counterproductive 'rap sessions?' "	"This is the reason that training is so important. By learning and using the proper skills, circle members will maximize every available moment to solve problems and create ideas. There won't be time for simply socializing."
"This program is a big investment. How can we be sure it will work?"	"We can't. But companies that have followed the strategy we have outlined for you have been tremendously successful. We are prepared to deal with any obstacle or mistake."

Figure 19. Objections to QCs and How to Counter Them

This discussion should not be allowed to continue endlessly. After a few minutes, it is a good idea to make a comment such as "If there are no more questions, we would like to ask once again for the 'go-ahead' for our plan. Do we have it?" Generally, either approval is conferred at this time, or the team is asked to wait until some thought can be given to the proposal. The possibility of the latter development should be anticipated, and in this event a summary emphasizing key points should be available to distribute to all present. It is essential, however, that everyone remain at the meeting until a firm date for an answer has been established.

PARTICIPANTS

Two groups of people attend the presentation. The team, of course, is one. As implied earlier, each member should have an assigned topic to research and explain. This, after all, is exactly the way in which the prospective circles will make their presentations to management.

In spite of this delegation of presentation assignments, a "patchwork" product need not result. At least one meeting of the team is required to synchronize the information, to select and design appropriate supporting materials (handouts, transparencies, graphs, and so forth), and to run one or more "dress rehearsals."

The second group is the audience, whose composition varies. In some cases the chief executive officer alone suffices, and in other cases all members of the highest level in the organization receive an invitation. It is important to address decision makers or at least those who have influence on the decision makers in the company.

The invitation to attend should be given with consideration for the time pressures that decision makers often face. Although the strategic plan is a top priority for the QC program, those to be invited are not yet aware of its importance. Thus, attendance at the meeting should be made attractive, and an R.S.V.P. should be requested.

TIME FRAME

The importance of total preparedness has been emphasized previously, and each team must judge for itself the amount of time required for such preparation. The actual presentation should take no more than an hour unless the senior managers who attend indicate a willingness to learn more. From the end of this session or from the time that approval of the plan is received, the team can expect to quicken its pace toward the actualization of quality circles in the company. Step 3 commences in approximately two to four weeks, and the pilot circles can begin in as little as three months.

TIPS FOR SUCCESS

The QC planner and the team should consider the following recommendations for making Step 2 a success.

- Be totally prepared.
- Know the audience. Predict the senior managers' comments and develop appropriate responses.
- Conduct at least one and as many as five dress rehearsals.
- Before the meeting send an informational article to the senior managers so that they will start thinking positively about the subject.
- Arrange the meeting room so that the presenters and the senior managers are combined. Seating the two groups on opposite sides of the room increases the perception of being on opposite sides of an idea.
- Recognize the senior managers' time pressures and express appreciation for their attendance at the presentation.
- Use attractive and descriptive visual aids.
- Maintain eye contact during delivery.
- Make every statement under the assumption that the project will proceed. Expect approval.
- Identify company supporters by name.
- Make sure that any question or objection is fully understood before an answer is given.
- Do not argue objections; hear them and respond professionally.
- Do not oversell. Present the case logically and confidently.
- Be honest; present all the facts.
- Do not keep "selling" if the senior managers unexpectedly grant early approval. Many salespeople become flustered when this happens because they have worked so diligently to prepare a complete presentation and do not want any of it to be "wasted."
- Be confident and the team will succeed.

"Selling" Quality Circles to Middle and Line Management

OVERVIEW

Although the "selling" process is basically the same for those in middle and line management and those who are union officials (and very similar to the senior-management "sale" of Step 2), the two "sales" are presented in different steps in order to cover the subtleties of each. A second reason for the division is that a significant number of readers are from nonunion environments and, therefore, are not interested in a discussion of union involvement in quality circles; consequently, these readers can omit Step 4. Step 3, however, covers a process that every organization must engage in when installing quality circles: "selling" the concept to middle and line managers.

Most behavioral scientists agree that the greatest resistance to change can be found in the middle levels of an organization. Why this is so is difficult to say. The answer may lie in the peculiar characteristics of the traditional hierarchy on which most modern organizations are built. However, it may just be that middle and line management attract people who resist change. For whatever reason, this tendency to resist must be recognized and given proper consideration in the activities of this step. The implementation team must understand that a single manager who feels threatened can sabotage a serious attempt to install QCs, even though the top executives are supportive of implementation.

The subtle process of politicking for support actually begins several weeks before Step 3. Although the word "politics" has a negative connotation in most companies, politicking is an essential and positive factor in QC implementation; in fact, the purpose of Step 3 is to formalize the support network that has been long in the making. It is true that senior management provides the foundation for a QC program; but middle and line management provide the necessary day-to-day support, and the implementation team begins to develop this support in another staged presentation during which the strategic plan and the reasons for installing quality circles are explained.

The objectives of this presentation are as follows:

- To generate positive acceptance of the plan;
- To reduce the managers' defensiveness and fear of the unknown;
- To provide a basic conceptual framework from which those in attendance can develop an understanding of QCs;
- To obtain the verbal commitment of at least three line managers to volunteer for the pilot project; and
- To define the roles that are to be played in the circle system.

The presentation should be brief (lasting an hour or so) and dynamic. Although attendance at the session should be voluntary, the team must also ensure a captive audience in order to achieve its mission. It is important to remember that the greater the turnout, the greater the team's chances of instilling enthusiasm and interest in each manager.

Middle and line managers typically put a low priority on spending valuable time hearing about a "new management technique." Most of them claim that they have far too many other things to do just in completing their work. Thus, the QC planner usually experiences this resistance even before he or she has a chance to tell the managers what QCs are all about.

The authors have found a simple yet effective way to overcome the strongest of objections to attending the presentation. The QC planner simply asks a newly made supporter from senior management to write and sign the invitation to the session. If the writer is well regarded and has a voice in what happens within the organization, the session automatically takes on greater importance to those invited.

It is assumed that since receiving senior-management approval to proceed, the implementation-team members have been determining the levels of resistance to and acceptance of the QC concept. In addition, they have been applying strategies to shift the balance of opinion at least to neutral, if not to total *commitment. This presentation offers the team an opportunity to solidify the support already gained as well as to make new allies. Since the time is limited, it must be well spent; the content description provides details on how to maximize the impact of the team's promotion.*

One last bit of advice is to give careful consideration to the following four levels of appeal:

Level I: The Bottom Line. *This is an arena of interest to any manager and is the easiest to address. A clear, concise statement of results achieved by other users of quality circles is sure to pique interest. It is important to offer specifics (Company X realized a $25,600 cost savings within a year) rather than generalities (quality circles have been known to give a 12-to-1 return on investment). It is also a good idea to give examples of moderate successes when measured by dollars saved or gained. Even though huge profit ideas (a quarter-million dollars or more) are generated by quality circles, they are far outnumbered by the thousands of smaller contributions that add up. For example, in Japan the average QC contributes fifty-five ideas or suggestions per member per year. Such a statistic needs little explanation.*

Level II: Actions Accomplished. *Although measurable, these actions appear distant from the bottom line. This category includes accomplishments that have to do with such managerial concerns as safety, levels of product or service quality, number of customer complaints, sales levels, and overall productivity measures. Again, the most effective approach is to offer examples of moderate achievements through quality circles and then allow the audience to draw its own conclusions.*

Level III: Communications and Industrial Relations. *This level, which is even further removed from Level I in terms of measurability, includes the areas of human interaction, power and influence, organizational climate, and employee morale. Because of the great difficulty in precisely defining the cause-and-effect relationships involved, managers often avoid issues related to these areas or assume that there is little that can be done to control them. The ability of QCs to affect such issues positively is difficult to "sell," and the team may encounter a critical point of resistance when it broaches this subject. Thus, the job involved, to be carried out with delicacy, is to convince the managers, without seeming to pressure, that quality circles are powerful tools for treating these intangibles. If a line manager can leave this meeting feeling that for once a way is known and available to spark some much-needed enthusiasm in a work unit, the design team will most assuredly have a convert to its cause.*

Level IV: Personal Sentiments. Levels I, II, and III are important targets, but none holds the potential for a "sale" that is found in the area of personal sentiments. A primary principle of sales is that the buyer must have a personal reason to make a purchase.

In order to prepare an effective presentation, the team must know the audience, determine possible personal reasons that the line managers might have for wanting to expend the time and effort to bring QCs into their work areas, and understand in what ways the idea of QCs might be perceived as threatening. In summary, it is essential to know and convey to the target managers the positive personal benefits that will accrue from QC implementation.

The authors have found that a carefully prepared presentation that addresses all four levels of appeal and offers the facts in a straightforward and dynamic manner results in a long roster of volunteers who are anxious to start circles in their own work areas. In fact, the majority of the line managers in the audience may well volunteer for the pilot project.

CONTENT

To "sell" the quality-circle concept to the company's middle and line managers, the team should use a format similar to that of the presentation to senior management. Only minor modifications are necessary.

A sample agenda includes the following topics:

- A definition of quality circles;
- Advantages and disadvantages of QCs;
- Budgetary considerations;
- The planning and implementation of QCs; and
- The role of line managers.

Each of these parts of the presentation is explained in detail in the following paragraphs.

1. *A Definition of Quality Circles.* The QC is described by using the same definition given to the senior-management group. A brief history of

the technique as well as a listing of local firms that use it can also be included.

2. *Advantages and Disadvantages of QCs.* This is the key agenda item for most managers. After QCs have been described, each member of the audience will try to picture them in operation in his or her work station. Doubts and fears about being successful will be foremost in every manager's mind. By sharing an extensive list of advantages and disadvantages, the team can speak directly to these fears. The list of disadvantages is a compilation of everything that can go wrong. When those in attendance realize that the negative aspects have been carefully considered, they will give the team credit for being able to counter them.

3. *Budgetary Considerations.* These matters are shared with this group for three reasons. The first is simply informational: to let the managers know that there is a budget and to give them its details. This sharing of information also accomplishes the second and third purposes: to indicate senior-management support and to show the professionalism of the implementation team.

4. *The Planning and Implementation of Quality Circles.* During this phase of the presentation, the QC planner briefly describes how he or she became involved with quality circles and offers the key points of the strategic plan, perhaps by letting the audience examine a milestone chart.

5. *The Role of Line Managers.* At this point Level-IV interests are addressed. The presenter should restate the plan for the pilot program, outline the team's criteria for selecting the most potential-filled areas for the initial circles, and clearly specify the managers' roles and projected time commitments. Woven through this presentation of facts should be the personal benefits that will accrue to those willing to enlist in the effort. The session can be concluded with the distribution of copies of the Interest Indicator (Figure 20) if the team feels that using this instrument is preferable to employing a sign-up list. The instrument approach allows the line managers to think about the ideas presented on their own time and avoids the communication of pressure on the team's part. As the instrument copies are distributed, the managers should be told when the team wants the forms returned and when it expects to make the decision about the pilot circles.

If the audience is obviously enthusiastic and ready to make commitments, it saves time to pass around a sign-up list immediately after concluding the presentation. In either case the team members should offer to make themselves available for further discussion and thank the managers for their time and attention.

Directions: Select and complete one of the three following alternatives.

1. Yes, I am interested in having a pilot quality circle in my area.

Name _____

Department _____ Extension _____

2. No, I am not interested for the following reasons(s): _____

_____

_____

_____

_____

_____

_____

3. I might be interested, but I would like additional information.

Name _____

Department _____ Extension _____

Figure 20. Interest Indicator

One critical issue that may be brought up during the course of the presentation is what to do with the cash benefits produced by the circles. This is a sensitive subject and must be handled with delicacy.

The authors know of QCs in some organizations that are rewarded with small cash amounts on a regular basis for results accomplished. They also know of other organizations that consider the recognition received by the circles to be a fair and sufficient return for circle efforts. Although both approaches have seemed to work thus far, it is likely that with any QC project a day will come when a circle member or two will add up all the cost savings achieved to date and will wonder how the recognition or the occasional bonus compares to the new "profits" being enjoyed by the organization or its shareholders. This awareness will spread, and the inevitable results will be discontent and resentment that are targeted directly at the circle program.

It is the authors' philosophy that true participative management means that all employees share not only in the responsibility for making decisions and solving problems, but also in the rewards that are reaped from their efforts. If the company already has a profit-sharing plan, a way should be found to work this plan into the QC system. If such a plan does not exist, the team must be prepared to face this issue during the presentation. Even if it does not come up at this time, it will certainly be raised later, either during the "sale" to the union or after the program has been implemented.

If the company has a system whereby employees are paid for suggestions, the system should be broadened to include QC suggestions. If this incorporation does not occur, the ideas that are developed in the circles will "mysteriously" find their way into the suggestion program. Such a development obviously inhibits the idea-generation willingness within the circles. In the authors' experience, including QCs in the paid-suggestion system encourages teamwork and allows the synergistic strength of QCs to blossom; not including them does just the opposite.

PARTICIPANTS

Depending on logistics, the team may want to include in the audience every area manager and supervisor, whether staff or line. Although most QC programs begin in production areas, quality circles work just as well to enhance indirect work efforts. Those units that are responsible for such indirect work may or may not be included in the pilots selected, but they should definitely be involved as the system expands throughout the organization.

The members of the implementation team are responsible for making the presentation. For best results, the team should recruit the official decision maker who wrote the invitation as a guest speaker and ask him or her to open the session by explaining the reason for the gathering and by saying a few words about why senior management has approved the project.

One more way to improve the team's influence is to identify beforehand the members of the audience who are known to be interested in quality circles. Invitations to these people should be delivered personally, along with a request to share their enthusiasm in the session. The more well spoken these individuals are, the greater will be their impact.

TIME FRAME

The presentation should last approximately an hour.

TIPS FOR SUCCESS

The following recommendations are provided for the team's consideration.

- Rechart the power of the organization (redo the Power Data Sheet and the Power Matrix, Figures 15 and 16, respectively, in Step 1). Know the audience beforehand.
- Overestimate the amount of time required by managers to start quality circles in their own areas.
- Use professional-looking visual aids that need little explanation.
- If possible, use the film "If Japan Can . . ." (see Step 2); it is very convincing.
- Ask particularly influential and supportive members of the audience to share their views.
- Make every statement under the assumption that the QC program will, in fact, be implemented. Essentially the presentation is being made because volunteers are needed for the pilot. Thus, the team should make the pilot a project that all line managers will want to join.
- Be fast and "hard hitting" in the presentation; give the managers credit for being able to draw their own conclusions.
- Refer to known supporters by name.
- Without actually saying so, assure the managers that quality circles do not threaten their power.
- Do not oversell. Quality circles make enough sense to convince any thoughtful manager.
- Do not belabor points. When the "sale" has been made, close.
- Do not become defensive when confronted with objections. Use the "I agree, but . . . " formula when responding and provide a logical counter (see Figure 19 in Step 2).
- Stress the need for a pilot group that is innovative and that has the capacity to deal with uncertainty as well as the ability to take risks. Most managers see the necessity for these characteristics.

- Let everyone know that senior managers will be visiting circles, monitoring results, and attending presentations from time to time.
- Offer to discuss the team's plan on a one-to-one basis with anyone who so desires.
- Encourage the interested line managers to talk with the employees in their areas to gauge interest levels. Emphasize the fact that this is a voluntary program.

"Selling" Quality Circles to the Union

OVERVIEW

The authors believe that without union concurrence no quality-circle program can survive, regardless of the support it receives from other sectors of the organization, regardless of abundant resources committed to it, regardless of the quality of the strategic plan, and regardless of the purity of the implementation team's motives. In a unionized organization employees wield a great deal of power through bargaining units.

Darwin's theory of evolution tells us that species adapt in order to survive the demands of their environments. This theory also holds true in the evolution of organizations and, subsequently, unions. In fact, it can be said that at one point, many years ago, unions were a natural result of intensely unpleasant organizational environments. The environment that formerly existed in many companies was one of harshness and abuse. Employees worked long hours in unclean and unsafe work places and received minimal wages for their labor. These conditions paved the way for unionization.

Although unions were developed for a logical purpose, they were born of conflict. The relationship between management and organized labor in most organizations is still, to some degree, adversarial. The authors' premise is that an adversarial relationship is counterproductive; much time and energy are required to sustain it, and these resources could be better spent in achieving the goals of the organization and its members. This is not to say that unions should be eliminated. On the contrary, they provide a valuable social structure as well as a formal means for communication between management and employees.

In Japan, although a large portion of the country's industry is unionized, the union involved tends to work collaboratively with management. It is this positive interface that sets the stage for the tremendous success enjoyed by QCs in Japan. American culture is certainly different from Japanese culture, and in this respect comparisons between American organizational life and that of Japan may seem invalid. Yet it seems obvious that we as a nation can no longer tolerate counterproductivity. Quality circles may well be the answer to changing this situation because they provide something for everyone.

In unionized settings the key to receiving the maximum voluntary participation of the work force is through the union. In fact, many unions treat the introduction of employee-participation programs like QCs as issues that can be bargained. They reason that such programs affect the working conditions within a company and are, therefore, subject to collective bargaining. Many labor agreements now include clauses to this effect.

To receive strong union support for a quality-circle program, two "concessions" are usually necessary. The first consists of sharing the credit for introducing the concept into the company with the union. The second consists of giving the union an ongoing, active way to monitor and add to the program, which can be accomplished by having union members serve on the steering committee.

Not all unions require both "concessions," but the strongest programs in the authors' experience include them. Through them the union's fear of being undermined by management is dispelled. When this happens, active union cooperation and support can be developed.

CONTENT

The "sale" made to the representatives of the company's union touches on the same four levels of appeal described in the overview of the "sale" to middle and line management in Step 3. Of course, the bottom line is defined differently in that union officials will probably demonstrate a greater concern for the benefits to be derived by those whom they represent. (The other levels will also have their differences for which the team should plan.)

Aside from these variances in the targets of appeal and the tendencies of the union audience to be smaller and the presentation more informal, an agenda similar to that proposed in Step 3 should be followed. An indication of interest is not necessary at the conclusion, but it is important to generate a commitment on the part of the union to play an active role in the implementation and ongoing reality of the circles. In this respect offering positions on the steering committee or even roles as area facilitators is a good place to start. The goal, of course, is to encourage union involvement rather than just observation. As discussed in the content of Step 3, the team should also be prepared to handle the subject of what is to be done with the monetary benefits produced by the circles; in fact, this issue is much more likely to be raised during the presentation to the union than it is during the session with the middle and line managers.

PARTICIPANTS

As already pointed out, the union presentation is conducted a bit differently from that for the middle and line managers. The authors suggest placing less emphasis on the decision-maker role and, because the team is dealing with a smaller audience in this case, conducting a round-table discussion in which two-way communication is encouraged when major points are being clarified. In comparison to the presentation made to middle and line management, the union session is much more informal.

It is advisable to use all or part of the implementation team and to invite the most influential union representatives, including officers and those from the areas most likely to sponsor the pilot circles. Once again, it is advantageous to identify supporters in advance and to ask them to say a few words.

TIME FRAME

Although the session may be scheduled for an hour, the team should allow plenty of time to continue as long as the union respresentatives have concerns or questions to voice.

TIPS FOR SUCCESS

Recommendations for successful completion of this step are as follows.

- Develop some knowledge and understanding of the audience before the meeting.
- Use effective visual aids.
- If possible, use the film "If Japan Can . . . " (see Step 2).
- Mention known supporters by name.

- Be careful not to oversell. Most union representatives are able to see the benefits inherent in QCs.
- Point out that quality circles give labor a significant role in decision making.
- Do not even hint that QCs are a technique for accelerating the work process. Quality circles enable people to work "smarter" rather than faster.
- When objections arise, avoid a defensive posture. As discussed in the previous step, use the "I agree, but . . . " formula.
- Mention that senior management plans to take an active role in the program by visiting circles, monitoring results, and attending occasional presentations.
- Indicate a willingness to discuss the QC plan further with any union representative who wants more information.

Selecting Pilots and Establishing Structure

OVERVIEW

Once the QC program has been officially "sold" to the key levels of the organization, the implementation team is ready to begin the actual installation. Step 5 entails not only selecting the pilot circles that will prove or disprove the validity of the strategic plan, but also instituting the QC structure designed weeks before in Step 1.

Several important questions must be answered in order to realize the planned QC structure.

- *Who is going to administer the program?*
- *Who will do the required training?*
- *Will a steering committee be formed?*
- *What roles will be played by the team members?*
- *Will the formal authority structure, as portrayed by the organizational hierarchy, determine circle leadership?*
- *Will a full-time, company-wide facilitator be employed, or will the facilitator role be assigned as an additional responsibility of one or more people in the organization?*
- *Who will manage communication between circles?*
- *How will managers be involved?*

Although the answers to most of these questions are covered in the strategic plan, there is a significant difference between answers on paper and their realization. It is the purpose of this step to bridge that gap.

One of the most crucial issues to be addressed is that of quality-circle coordination. The most popular structure for achieving coordination of circle efforts is the QC steering committee. Normally this committee is composed of upper-level managers, some area supervisors, the company facilitator(s), and occasionally the house personnel or human-resource specialist and/or a circle member. Steering-committee membership is determined by the design team. If it is decided that such a committee should exist, its composition must reflect the unique characteristics of the organization and the QC program it serves.

Another way to design the quality-circle system is to dispense with the steering committee and instead assign all of the committee's work to the QC administrator. In this case the position of administrator becomes a full-time job, and the person who performs it must be an expert in the general concept as well as in the special features of the team's strategic plan. The authors' preference is for a steering committee, whose members can provide ongoing support for the program throughout the company in their varied capacities.

Training, as emphasized repeatedly in this book, is a very important part of quality circles. The process of training is discussed in detail in Step 6, but it should be known at this point that during Step 5 decisions must be made about the system for delivering this training. Because quality circles are based on the idea of maximizing the use of available human resources, this theme might readily be carried out when the team engages in training design and delivery.

If the company is fortunate enough to have an in-house trainer or training staff, the team should tap this valuable resource. Company trainers can be given the full responsibility for design and delivery, or they can be asked to coach those who will be responsible.

Another viable source for training is the increasing number of consulting and/or training firms that offer training packages, and utilization of this source is discussed thoroughly in the next step. At this point it is sufficient to say that the team's approach to training will mold the QC structure as it becomes established.

One of the most important and potentially "touchy" decisions that the team must make involves the future responsibilities of its own members, who have worked so diligently in designing the project implementation. This decision is referred to as "touchy" because the authors' experience is that those on the implementation team have been living day in and day out with this exciting adventure and, almost unanimously, wish to remain integral parts of the structure they designed. This is not always possible in exactly the way they envision. The best approach to smoothing out the disbanding of the implementation team is to make sure that a consensual agreement as to future roles is reached during the strategic-planning session. It is also essential to ensure that recognition of the members' efforts in creating quality circles is both plentiful and ongoing. Years after implementation, when someone inquires as to how the program began, the collective organizational memory should quickly produce the names of these individuals. Securing this type of recognition increases the team members' sense of satisfaction.

For expediency and to minimize the defensiveness of middle and line managers, the authors favor an initial program structure that is somewhat parallel to the official hierarchy defined by the organizational chart. In other words, the circle leaders are the supervisors of the individual work groups; the steering-committee members are from middle management and above; and the circle members are the employees who perform the actual work.

Although many QC programs adhere to this initial structure, they are usually quick to deviate from the traditional order of getting things done as both managers and workers begin to see the potential for leadership that lies, to some extent, in every member of the organization. An extremely valuable but often unrecognized and certainly unplanned-for side effect of quality circles is the development of the skills and characteristics of leadership in every participant. Ultimately this development strengthens the organization.

The structure commonly begins to deviate from that of the organizational chart in companies in which the span of control is broad. For example, a QC in a work area in which an individual supervises twenty or more workers gradually infects nonmembers with its enthusiasm and its desire to accomplish, and these nonmembers subsequently raise a demand for the opportunity to participate in a circle. Obviously, the supervisor cannot lead two, three, or more circles because of time constraints. The solution to this dilemma is to have the supervisor establish a new circle and appoint as its leader a capable member of the veteran circle or simply allow the new circle to choose its own leader. Another form of leadership structure that is gaining in popularity is alternating leadership: Every member of the circle is given the leadership responsibility for a predetermined period of time, at the end of which another member assumes the role. In any case, the implementation team's job is to establish the initial structure and then let the individual circles work out their own forms of direction.

Another structural concern mentioned earlier is the question of circle facilitation. The section of Step 5 entitled "Participants" describes in greater detail the role of a QC facilitator. At this point it is sufficient to state that a facilitator is the key coordinating and training resource for the circles. So important is this role in the ongoing activities of quality circles that the authors have yet to discover a company that does not have one or more facilitators, whether or not this term is used to designate the position.

The options regarding the structure of the facilitator's job are numerous and range from the creation of a formal QC-facilitating department with an extensive staff, a spot on the organizational chart, and a working budget to an informal system in which interested managers volunteer their time and energy to carry out the facilitator role.

There are options in terms of the number of facilitators as well. Some organizations find that a single individual can carry out the duties of the position for the total roster of circles. Others assign facilitator responsibility to several individuals, each with a limited number of circles to oversee. One of the authors' client organizations decided to train the manager of each area as a facilitator to his or her own circles, which, in turn, were led by the supervisors who reported to the manager.

The particular structure that is chosen is a reflection of the organization it serves. Regardless of its form, the structure of the quality-circle project must provide for communication between upper management and circle members and among the circles themselves. Communication not only ensures recognition of circle achievements, but also prevents duplication of effort. Examples of the many ways used to dispense information that is critical to the ongoing success of the program include newsletters, company conferences, open-invitation presentations to management, and circle meetings to which guests are invited.

While these and several other issues pertaining to the proposed structure are being actualized, another crucial action is being carried out: selection of the areas in which the first circles in the organization will be instituted. These pilot circles *will determine, for better or worse, the quality of the strategic plan and the viability of the QC concept in the organization. The importance of making a very careful and deliberate choice of start-up circles is obvious.*

During the discussion of Step 3, it was suggested that copies of the Interest Indicator (Figure 20) be distributed at the conclusion of the "sale" to the middle and line managers. When the team is ready to begin Step 5, the completed forms should be available so that a list of work areas that have volunteered for the pilot project can be compiled.

In evaluating the list for the selection of a maximum of three sites for start-up circles, the team should look carefully for certain characteristics that the authors have identified as vital to pilot success. The areas chosen should offer a high potential for cost savings, quality improvements, and/or productivity increases. In addition, the personal traits of each area manager should be considered; the managers of the selected areas should have a reputation for innovativeness, the ability to take calculated risks, and a leadership style that leans toward McGregor's (1960) Theory Y (as explained in the section entitled "The Circle Motivational Basis" in Part I).

CONTENT

Selecting Pilots

When making the selection of pilot circles, the team should attempt to match as closely as possible the characteristics of the work areas and the members with the suggested criteria. If the presentation to the middle and line managers has been effective, the list of volunteer areas is lengthy and must be pared down to the two or three that seem most appropriate for initiating the effort.

The most important criterion for selecting the pilot areas is the type of leadership style that exists in the immediate work place. Areas in which supervisors demonstrate some elements of a participative-management style should be chosen. Typically such supervisors have already established good personal relationships with their subordinates and have learned how to include them in the decision-making process. They accept suggestions and, because of their participative style, have developed some talent at working with the group-interaction process. These traits increase their chances of establishing effective circles; whether they realize it or not, supervisors who exhibit these characteristics do so because of their basic

Theory-Y (McGregor, 1960) belief in people. To become successful in the pilot effort, these leaders primarily need the structure and support provided by the QC program and a fundamental knowledge of the statistical tools used by circles.

Conversely, authoritarian supervisors, who do not agree with and/or understand the principles behind participative management, must rethink their management philosophies if they are to become effective circle leaders. This process does not happen overnight; sometimes it never happens. Unless it does, however, this type of supervisor is unable to establish an effective QC in which the members are committed to solving problems, reducing costs, and developing innovations.

There are many ways to help determine the present style of supervisory leadership.

- Observation at the work place;
- Observation during supervisor-led meetings;
- Interviews with the supervisor and his or her manager;
- Group discussions in a half-day or full-day session with potential leaders;
- Interviews with the supervisor's work group (conducted with the permission of the supervisor); and
- Questionnaires or other instruments designed to identify Theory-X or Theory-Y beliefs.

Determining whether or not a directive supervisor can become an effective QC leader is more complicated. Usually directive leaders have developed their styles for one of two reasons: Either they are philosophically closer to Theory-X beliefs than they are to Theory-Y beliefs, or their work groups have demonstrated that a directive style is necessary to accomplish the work objectives. A fine distinction is involved here in the sense that one can cause the other; because of the power of expectations (the "self-fulfilling prophecy"), Theory-X supervisors can foster Theory-X behavior in their work groups, thereby confirming their original beliefs.

To reverse this process it is necessary to proceed slowly and encourage such supervisors to develop trust in their subordinates gradually. Although reversal is difficult, it can be accomplished if the supervisors are willing to try. Some are not willing, and these individuals will never make effective QC leaders.

The work group can assist a supervisor in making this transformation in leadership styles. In one of the authors' client organizations, for example, the pilot program began with three circles. One of the carefully selected supervisors emerged as a highly authoritarian, Theory-X leader. She tightly controlled the first few meetings, lectured most of the time, and sat at one end of the room while the "class" sat at the other. The authors were invited to attend one of her early sessions and were concerned by what they witnessed, but after several long discussions decided not to do anything about the situation. One of the early tenets adopted for the program was that there must be room for failure on the part of everyone involved; the program had been "sold" to the company's executives in an open and candid manner, and this point had been stressed.

The authors knew, however, that the training modules were designed to stimulate teamwork, creativity, and participation in the overall context of group achievement. During this initial training, each circle is encouraged to select a simple, cost-saving project and to learn the statistical tools while working on the project. This approach allows beginning circles to relate what they are learning to what they have experienced in the work place. It also allows the members to focus on something outside the circle process and the numerous statistical techniques. Three other advantages accrue: The circles experience success early; they undergo the experience of making a presentation to management within weeks; and the overall program is given important impetus when these early results are reported.

This entire training process quickly highlights the value of a quality circle, whose major strength is synergistic. All of the members working together can accomplish more than each person working alone. When an autocratic supervisor reaches this conclusion, the battle is nearly won. In the example just described, this is what gradually happened to the struggling supervisor. She began to realize that she could not succeed without the group's cooperation. When the members began coming to circle meetings with critical information and began suggesting valuable ideas, her style began to change; she began to encourage participation. The self-imposed pressure of the group's upcoming presentation to management also gave the members a reason to work together—they did not want to be embarrassed.

The combined result of these factors was an effective QC led by a supervisor who had learned the personal and bottom-line value of participative management. At the end of the group's first presentation to management, in the presence of the company president and other top officials, the circle members presented the supervisor with a gift as a token of their appreciation.

The primary reason for sharing this experience is not to delude the reader into believing that every circle will be successful. Instead, the example is presented to highlight the following points:

- Even when using the best criteria available, it is impossible to predict with 100-percent accuracy how a supervisor will react in a circle setting.

- Sometimes the best course of action to take with a struggling circle is to let it struggle.
- The synergism that develops in most circles is a powerful force.
- Directive supervisors can change their styles if they see a personal reason for doing so (that is, to achieve success).

The remaining criteria for selecting the pilot-circle areas—the potential for improvement and the innovativeness and risk-taking ability of the supervisors involved—are less important than the issue of demonstrated leadership styles.

Usually the areas that actually return the greatest savings through circle efforts are those that are already run efficiently. Although this may seem to be a contradiction of QC principles, it has been the case in many programs. The authors think this is true because the employees in these efficiently run work areas are better disciplined in their daily efforts and understand their work processes to a greater degree than employees in wasteful units. This comprehension allows them to pinpoint bottlenecks quickly and then develop workable solutions and suggestions.

The risk-taking ability of supervisors can be gauged by their involvement in other activities within the company. Answering some of the following questions helps in judging whether a supervisor possesses this ability.

- Does the supervisor participate in any teams sponsored by the company?
- Does he or she do any public speaking?
- Does the supervisor volunteer for special committees?
- Does he or she hold any offices in outside organizations?
- Has the work area of the supervisor changed recently?
- Has the supervisor ever suggested changes in the work process?

Although the process of answering these questions is subjective, the authors believe that positive answers tend to indicate an ability and willingness to take risks and to innovate. Other indicators will be developed as the team progresses, but these criteria provide a starting point for making the best decision possible.

If the team has done an exceptionally good job of generating enthusiasm among middle and line managers, the final selection may be difficult. There is always the possibility of hurt feelings among those whose areas are not selected. Part of the selection process is the communication of the final decision to everyone concerned. The team must be prepared to meet face to face with every manager and/or supervisor whose area was not chosen and to describe the selection process candidly. These managers should be assured that their areas have not been eliminated as potential QCs, but that as soon as the pilot is evaluated and proven a success, they will be contacted to join in the expansion program. It might be wise to note one particular benefit of not being selected for the pilot: The first circles make a lot of mistakes that the second generation of circles will be able to avoid.

Establishing QC Structure

The establishment of a QC structure is more involved than the selection of pilot circles; many more tasks and activities must be completed. The following list is extensive and can easily be converted to a check list with the team's additions or deletions so that it makes sense for the specific program. There is no particular order suggested in this listing.

- Select a steering committee.
- Select a QC administrator.
- Develop written QC role descriptions.
- Meet with selected pilot supervisors to brief them.
- Meet individually with nonselected volunteers.
- Decide on a company communication vehicle.
- Decide on possible QC deviations (such as "co-circles, "mini-circles," intra-organizational circles, and so forth as described in Step 9).
- Start a recruiting campaign for circle members.
- Determine the use of and requirements for the facilitator(s).
- Select the facilitator(s).
- Determine the company QC policy.
- Conduct climate testing to ascertain the level of acceptance of QCs.
- Determine the in-house resources that are available.
- Determine the availability of external expertise.
- Write manuals of operation for the steering committee, the administrators, the facilitator(s), the leaders, and the members.
- Select volunteers who will be circle members.
- Phase out or involve in other ways the members of the implementation team.
- Ask managers and the steering-committee members to commit to the attendance of a certain number of presentations to management.
- Establish a record-keeping procedure for achievements.

- Write a company charter and goals for quality circles (if they have not already been written).
- Communicate all actions to everyone concerned.
- Establish a meeting schedule for the steering committee.

PARTICIPANTS

Normally at this point in the development of a circle system, the QC planner and the implementation team are still actively involved in laying the foundation described in the strategic plan. In some cases, however, this responsibility has been turned over to or assumed in collaboration with the newly formed steering committee, the company QC administrator, and/or the program facilitator(s). If this transition has not yet been accomplished, it should be before the next step is undertaken (unless, of course, the QC planner and the design team are the focal points of responsibility for the project).

The following paragraphs briefly describe several of the roles that come into play in this step of implementation:

1. *Steering-Committee Member.* This person is usually a member of mid- to upper-level management who meets on a regular basis with other such managers representing every QC-participating function and area of the organization. The steering committee is responsible for establishing policy and procedure; approving large-scale recommendations and requests for circle funds; participating in management presentations; and, in general, giving the company's QC program a direction.

2. *Administrator.* This individual is selected to work part- or full-time on the responsibilities of coordination, communication, and paperwork required by quality circles.

3. *Facilitator.* This role is fulfilled by a person who works part- or full-time with one or more circles (and perhaps all circles in the company) to solve operational problems, to help in preparation for management presentations, to obtain supplies and resources, to train circle leaders, and to serve as an information resource.

4. *Circle Leader.* This person, usually the area supervisor, has been specially trained to both train and lead a single circle. Leadership of circle activities is noncontrolling and nonauthoritarian; the leader keeps the group on track and acts as a resource for directions in problem solving.

5. *Circle Member.* A circle's membership is its most important element. The individual member is a full-time participant in the work of the area and has volunteered to take part in the circle. Voluntary participation is critical in that it guarantees a degree of commitment to

the decisions and actions that are the result of the circle process. Once an employee joins the circle in the area, he or she is trained, given more training, and then retrained. When the member becomes skilled in using the statistical methods and tools to be employed so often in the circle's life, still more training is provided. The continual development of self and the maximization of potential are the primary goals for each member.

6. *Consultant.* If the team opts for a consultant, the individual chosen must have experience in the complexities involved in selecting pilot circles and developing the QC structure. Although the information and advice offered by the consultant should be considered carefully, the final decisions must be made by the team.

TIME FRAME

Within a week or two following the presentations to middle and line management and to the union (if applicable), the team should be sufficiently prepared to proceed with the tasks of establishing the QC structure and making the selection of pilots. Once this step has been accomplished, the fully functioning circle system that has been planned is nearly a reality. After the basic training described in Step 6 has been completed, the pilots will begin confronting work problems, reducing costs, and generating innovative ideas. If all goes well, the team is only ten to fifteen weeks from this milestone.

TIPS FOR SUCCESS

The following recommendations apply to this step.

- Include decision makers on the steering committee.
- Start with a single pilot circle and implement a maximum of one or two others within the first six months.
- Ask those supervisors or managers who volunteer for the pilot project to begin thinking of goals and objectives for their circles.
- Select pilot circles from areas that have maintained positive records of past production.
- Select as the first circle leaders those managers or supervisors who are innovative, able to take risks, and willing to make mistakes.
- To avoid disappointment, inform everyone that the first circles are only pilots and that they will be followed by others.

- Make certain that the pilot circles understand that their projects should be related to their work.
- Use the existing organizational structure as a model for the QC structure.
- Establish and communicate goals against which the pilots may later be measured.
- Develop and distribute to everyone involved a charter that clearly spells out the roles and lines of authority in the circle system.
- Implement a data-gathering and information-sharing procedure that includes reporting forms to keep track of circle activities and accomplishments.
- Consider a QC newsletter for the company.

REFERENCE

McGregor, D. *The human side of enterprise*. New York: McGraw-Hill, 1960.

Training

OVERVIEW

As has been emphasized repeatedly, strategic planning is the most important step in the authors' model. Without the solid foundation and sure direction that a plan provides, the QC program will most likely flounder. Another critical element is the QC structure, through which the plan is implemented. However, one vital component without which no progress can be made in spite of the most concisely outlined strategic plan and the most carefully developed QC structure is training. It is training that keeps the program moving steadily toward the goal of a more productive and effective organization.

An obviously unique feature of quality circles in comparison with other schemes for productivity improvement is the strong emphasis on extensive training for members of every level of the organization. The major audiences of QC training and the types of instruction they receive are described as follows:

- *Employees who participate as circle members learn the skills of systematic problem solving.*
- *Line managers are trained in actual circle-leadership roles.*
- *Facilitators are trained in ways to assist circles in achieving maximum effectiveness.*
- *The organization's middle managers are trained in the concepts and support of circles.*

Before looking further at the training needs of these audiences, it is wise to examine the options available when selecting the sources of training designs and materials. The choices range from the purchase of an off-the-shelf training package to the complete design of an in-house program. There are certain advantages and disadvantages to the different approaches.

Off-the-shelf packages are the most popular training choice with American QC implementers. The number of vendors of such packages is still limited at this time, but is growing steadily. Most packaged programs include lessons on cassette tapes, slide presentations and transparencies, training guides, workbooks, and manuals. Some even come with a consultant-trainer who facilitates the pilot training. Quality ranges from fair to good, and the price, when considered as a one-time investment, is reasonable. What is available in packages can be determined by looking through any recent journal from the fields of management, human resources, personnel, or training to find advertisements. If the organization decides to purchase a package, the advantages of this approach include time savings, reasonable pricing, easy implementation, and professional-quality materials. There are also problems associated with this choice, however, of which the team should be aware. Although most of the authors' clients have used off-the-shelf training materials, their satisfaction has not been complete. In fact, a sizable portion of the authors' QC work is in the area of rewriting and tailoring these packages for companies that have stumbled over the obstacles inherent in packaged training.

Most packages now available were designed for the aerospace industry, which was the first to "import" quality circles. It is true that the basic statistical tools presented in these packages are the same for circles in any organization. However, the examples used are presented in the context of the aerospace industry and are unsuitable and difficult to understand and apply for brewery workers or insurance-claim representatives. One way to solve this problem is to substitute examples from the appropriate industry wherever possible.

Another complaint often heard from companies that use packages is that the material is geared to a level too low to keep the trainees challenged and attentive. Like television programs, these packages have been designed to meet the learning capacity of the "lowest common denominator." Students in QC training programs are necessarily "tracked" rather than trained according to their individual abilities. The result is that medium to fast learners find the material to be less than challenging.

Frequently a simple concept is repeated over and over again. For example, in one packaged program reviewed by the authors, the process of brainstorming, an important QC tool, was well presented at the beginning of training. However, it was reviewed nine times throughout the rest of the package. The purpose in doing this may be to assure the conceptualization of the tool; but the result is trainee resentment and impatience, and a resentful, impatient learner is not an effective learner. This problem can be partially resolved by eliminating the redundancies wherever possible by discarding a slide or throwing away a work sheet.

A third problem in packages is their pace. A professional trainer knows that every individual learns at his or her own rate, a fact that makes the training of groups a real challenge. Inherent in audio-visual, programed training is its inflexibility in adapting to the learning speed of individual trainees. If the circle leader has skill in training others, he or she will be alert to the signals from members and will adjust the pace accordingly by viewing the parts of training as modules with no time limit. The outline that comes with a package should be used as a guideline rather than an absolute directive for the delivery of training.

One alternative to packaged training programs is in-house design and delivery. This approach can be carried out by internal trainers and instructional designers, if they are available; by an external consultant with expertise in this area; or by a combination of the two. A wealth of benefits accrues to the organization that selects this option. The first of these is the fact that a custom-designed training program reflects the issues and problems that are particular to the organization and its work. Thus, trainees easily find a common base of understanding. In addition, companies that design their own training commonly make use of employees as "actors" in the audio-visuals, which is another way to connect with the training audience. Interest and enthusiasm run high when trainees recognize their co-workers in training slides. An internally designed and delivered training program can also incorporate examples of problems or costs that the trainees deal with on a regular basis. Again, trainees are inspired to participate in the study of the QC tools when they can be applied to an issue of personal concern.

No two quality circles, even within the same organization, are identical in their goals, objectives, or maturity rate. A customized, modular training format gives each circle the freedom it needs to approach problem solving in its own unique way. At any given point, the circle trainer—usually the leader—can choose the module that is most appropriate to the circle's immediate situation. Another advantage to internal training design is that delivery can be geared to allow the easy addition or deletion of materials without harming the overall structure of the program.

Still another alternative approach is a combination of packaged and customized training. The special advantage to this selection is that the reinvention of basic techniques is avoided and the unique needs of the organization are addressed at the same time.

The organization's choice of a training source depends on many factors, including the availability of internal expertise, the numbers of people to be trained, the time available for training, the financial resources available, and personal preferences. The authors' preference is to use customized training because of the uniqueness of every organization. However, the primary disadvantage of developing customized training is the time required to design and write appropriate material; these tasks can rarely be accomplished in a period of less than two months.

Many firms have hired consultants who have existing QC training modules that can be customized for the client. This process can usually be completed within a few weeks.

An additional consideration of which the reader should be aware is that very little is available in the way of advanced training. Training for quality circles is not a one-time effort but an ongoing activity. Once the members of a circle master the basic statistical tools of problem solving, they will want to learn new, more complex processes for more complex projects. They will also want to increase their competence in group participation and platform delivery. Consequently, new ideas and new training modules will be required. Internally designed training is the best alternative as circles mature. Everyone involved in the program should be encouraged to suggest new topics for training modules.

CONTENT

As mentioned in the "Overview," several separate groups receive QC training. This section identifies the content of training required for each.

Circle Members

The first and most basic type of training for members involves the application of quality-circle tools. These tools are used continually throughout the life of the circle, and they consist of the statistical methods that have been used in business and industry for most of the Twentieth Century. The difference that QCs have introduced is that these tools are used by the employees who perform the work rather than by the engineers, managers, or specialists who oversee it.

The basic tools that are usually included in the first phase of such training are as follows:

- Brainstorming;
- Data-collection devices (such as check lists);
- Pareto analysis;[4]
- Cause-and-effect diagrams;
- Data-display techniques (including histograms, charts, graphs, and so forth);
- Sampling; and
- Techniques for determining costs.

The objective of training in the use of these tools is to develop the ability of each circle member to select the most appropriate tool for a particular set of circumstances and then to apply it correctly. This ability requires the talent to understand the dynamic processes of solving problems, reducing costs, and exploiting opportunities.

In training circle members, it is critical to present the QC process and the tools together. It may seem more efficient to offer one tool at a time and to practice its use in a variety of cases, but the hoped-for objective is lost with this approach. The authors have found that the most effective training agenda is similar to the one presented in Figure 21.

The problem-solving process, which is illustrated in Figure 22, presents more than one route from which to choose for each step involved. The circle members rediscover this phenomenon with each new problem they try to solve. The same is true for projects involving cost savings and innovation. By becoming familiar with the tools while actually working on

---

[4]When applied to QCs, Pareto analysis (Slaybough, 1966) is a technique whereby circle members can identify the most important issues to deal with in order to realize maximum payoff for their efforts. In this way they are able to recognize the "vital few" projects and, thus, avoid the "trivial many."

- Introduction to problem solving: an overview of the process
- Identifying a problem
  —Brainstorming as a way to determine possible problems
  —Practicing brainstorming
  —Clarifying and condensing a brainstorm list: discussion skills
  —Practicing clarifying and condensing
  —Pareto analysis: separating the vital few
  —Practicing Pareto
  —Narrowing down the list to one problem project: consensus
- Data gathering
  —Using a check list, sampling, a cause-effect diagram, or a similar device
  —Practicing data gathering
- Selecting a solution
  —Practicing the generation of alternatives
  —Decision testing and Pareto for alternatives
  —Practicing the analysis of alternatives
  —Selecting from alternatives
- Planning for implementation and predicting outcomes
  —Practicing planning and predicting
- Implementing and evaluating
  —Practicing the evaluation of results
- Presenting outcomes: preparing charts, histograms, graphs, tables, transparencies, and so forth
  —Practicing preparation for presentation
- Conducting presentation

Figure 21. Sample Learning Agenda for the QC Process and QC Tools

---

simple projects, the members gradually acquire the knowledge necessary to be able to use the correct tool at the appropriate time.

Another focus of member training is less tangible, but just as important as the tools. This is the understanding of the process and dynamics of group interaction. Quality circles cannot be mistaken for the traditional "meetings" or "committees" with which we all are familiar. Instead, QCs are based on a style of interaction between people that is an innovation for most organizations. Their consensual and egalitarian nature is very different from the structure and conduct of other groups to which most Americans

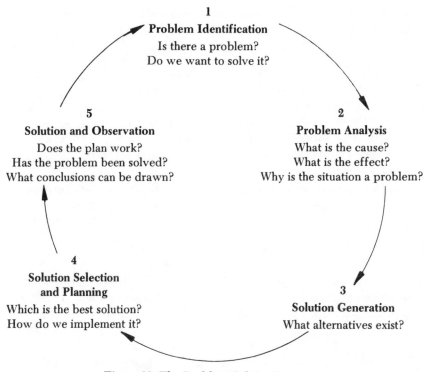

Figure 22. The Problem-Solving Process

belong. Therefore, the circle member must develop a broad comprehension of how the human being behaves in an unstructured group. This can best be accomplished by offering the members an opportunity to observe themselves in the context of the circle. Important elements of introductory circle training include the topics of teamwork, consensus in decision making, and creativity.

The authors have discovered that the understanding of group behavior is correlated positively with the quality of the projects engaged in and the problems solved by circles. Although there is a great deal of literature on the subject of group behavior, circles do not have the time to commit to a comprehensive study of the field. The authors have also learned, somewhat painfully, that circles do not benefit from learning by rote the basic theories and definitions.

In the first QC-training programs that the authors designed, they included a lesson on group process in which the circle leader delivered a lecturette on common behavioral styles found in groups. The members then participated in a short group experience and subsequently were asked to analyze their own styles of behavior within the group. This lesson was entertaining, but it failed to bring about any significant incorporation of new, more productive and collaborative group behaviors.

The authors have since made several changes in this aspect of member training. The overriding goal of training in group process became not a cognitive knowledge of the facts, but a deeply felt psychological under-standing of behavioral principles resulting in observable changes in the way each individual functions in the group. Furthermore, if the training was effective, these changes would be in the direction of a greater ability to listen to and hear others, to withhold judgment in considering the issues, and to participate collaboratively in the quest of group goals and objectives.

Consequently, the authors now devote the first two or three sessions of circle training to the topics of teamwork and consensual decision making. They begin with a brief lecturette on the difference between a collaborating team and a democratic committee and conclude with a clear statement of their objective: to help the trainees to become familiar and comfortable with a consensual way of participating in a group.

Trainees can experience this difference by participating in a group activity. A structured experience such as "Wilderness Survival: A Consensus-Seeking Task"[5] is an effective choice, or the group may accomplish something as simple as the rank ordering of possible outcomes of circle membership.

For the first phase of the activity, the participants should be told only to complete the chosen task in as short a time as possible by using whatever method (chosen leader, voting, and so forth) they wish. When the activity has been completed, it is critiqued by recording each participant's satisfaction and agreement with the outcome. A few words in conclusion from the circle leader help to point out the correlation between the degree of satisfaction and agreement with a group decision and the consequent level of commitment to it.

The second phase of the activity should be introduced with a brief lecturette on the necessity of active listening in a group decision-making experience. The participants are then instructed to complete the same task in the shortest time possible by achieving a consensus. They are told to use active-listening skills such as reflection and clarification before making statements of their own and to adhere to the following principles governing consensual discussion and decision making:

---

[5]From D.T. Simpson, "Wilderness Survival: A Consensus-Seeking Task," in J.W. Pfeiffer and J.E. Jones (Eds.), *The 1976 Annual Handbook for Group Facilitators*, University Associates, 1976.

- The decision must be one with which every member can live.
- No voting or bargaining is allowed.
- Every member must have the opportunity to express his or her opinion and reasons for it.
- No member may state that the opinions of another member are "wrong."
- No lobbying is allowed.

Once again, after completion the process is critiqued. Commonly, although the participants spend approximately twice as much time completing the second phase of the activity, they tend to enjoy it more and to feel more satisfied with the process and the solution. Later, when discussing the entire experience, they generally agree that the extra time required for arriving at a consensus is worth it in order to achieve a resolution of high quality that provides personal satisfaction to everyone in the group. If the learning experience is successful, the circle is on its way to developing solid norms for group interaction that will promote cohesiveness, integration, esprit de corps, and productivity in its efforts.

Norms, the unspoken rules for group behavior to which members subscribe, are a topic of relevance to circle training. The authors find it useful to define norms by giving simple examples and then asking the members to share the norms that are used in their families or social groups. A discussion may follow in which the members identify the norms that would contribute to the success of a QC.

Another element of introductory training involves speaking before a group, a task that has been identified by many authorities as the greatest common fear. This subject must be dealt with in training because the ability to express oneself in and before a group is a key part of the circle problem-solving process.

As stated previously, a circle obtains part of the recognition that feeds its spirit by making presentations to management. These presentations are formal, "staged" showcases of circle activities, resolutions, and recommendations. The circle members deliver their presentations to an audience composed of one or more managers and others who will be affected by the changes that the circle suggests. At least four times a year, each circle gathers its data and designs a presentation, sometimes to inform and sometimes to "sell" a recommended solution. The presentation usually consists of a description of the problem-identification process that the QC followed, charts and graphs that succinctly portray the important data collected, and a logical outline of the suggested solution.

The skill of effective delivery is the first and foremost of those required in presentations to management. Because most QC members have rarely had the opportunity to speak before an audience in a formal setting, some instruction in presentation style and technique is necessary. One of the most effective ways to develop this skill is through the use of modern technology. If the organization has access to a videotape recording system, circle members will be able to observe themselves as they perform in a dress rehearsal. Learning comes more easily when self-critique is the primary form of feedback. However, such equipment is not an absolute necessity. By the time that the topic of management presentations is reached in the course of training, the circle will have evolved into a close-knit team. Each member will be able to contribute an objective evaluation and positive suggestions for the improvement of a fellow member's delivery. The members themselves are the circle's most valuable resource.

Eventually, one or more members of every circle will emerge as the "best" public speakers. If all are in agreement, these members can serve as the primary presenters. There are plenty of other roles to be filled and tasks to be completed in making a clear, interesting presentation to management.

One of the crucial jobs is the design and development of the visual aids, which may include transparencies, posters and charts, written handout materials, and simple flip charts. The artistic skills of circle members should be tapped to develop these supports. If the organization is fortunate enough to have an art department, it can be a valuable resource in this aspect of training. A few members may take on the permanent role of circle artists. If they can do the job, this is an excellent idea. One of the basic purposes of a quality circle is to encourage the unique contribution of each member's ideas, skills, and talents.

In summary, circle members learn to function effectively in a group, to apply statistical methods to problems and issues in their work, and to present their findings to management. These learnings occur both in formal instruction and in the context of group work, and the members continually develop their skills through both.

Circle Leaders

Everything that a circle member knows must be known to a greater extent by the circle leader. This requirement is critical because it is the circle leader who is responsible for training the members in the skills and abilities just described. Therefore, one important aspect of the leader's training deals with how to be an effective trainer.

The training of trainers is a broad subject that must be condensed in order to highlight the most salient points for circle leaders. The first and most basic of these points is that the trainer must clearly understand the principles of adult learning. One of the greatest mistakes that a neophyte trainer makes is to teach in the manner in which he or she was taught as a schoolchild. This approach is simply not effective. The greatest difference between a child and an adult in the realm of learning is the fact that adults, unlike children, have years of experience to draw on. This fact should be stressed, along with the following related principles:

- Adults learn more readily when an understandable objective has been communicated and accepted.
- Adult learning is precipitated when the learners can relate new concepts to real situations in their lives.
- Although adults are tolerant of nonparticipative, "learn-by-listening" teaching, their learning is more effective when they have the opportunity to experience as well as to hear.
- Adults learn more quickly when they value the effect of learning or, in other words, the newly learned behavior.
- Adult learning is most likely to occur when the learner can make use of his or her unique set of life experiences.
- Adults can operate in and learn from unstructured, ambiguous situations from which they are able to draw their own conclusions.

Each circle leader should be given an outline to follow in the training of the circle's members. However, individual interpretations of the methods to be used will inevitably arise. This is fully acceptable as long as the leader pays heed to the precepts just stated. Because of the very nature of QC training, one step will not necessarily follow another. Thus, a second major point to be highlighted is that the leader is responsible for selecting the next step that fits best with what the group is trying to accomplish. Because there is no set pattern in the project course, it is important for the trainer to know fully the applications of all the available tools so that the appropriate action can be taken.

A third point to be made in this discussion of trainer training is that the circle leader must become proficient in the use of several different types of learning aids, which include, but are not limited to, artifacts, models, simulations, case studies, audiovisuals, charts and pictorials, videotape, role play, demonstration, discussion, and so forth. Of course, many of these, in particular the visuals, will be made available to the leader as a part of the training package. The leader must be encouraged to make use of the aids that best fit his or her situation and personal training style. Too often the authors have seen leaders fall into the trap of following their training guides to the letter and hiding behind an overhead projector. This behavior is probably attributable to nervousness and a temporary lack of training confidence. In any case, this is not effective and must be prevented. One way to avoid this situation is to require leaders in training to design their own skeletal versions of member-training packages. As part of this task they can be asked to develop case studies, transparencies, and other aids of their choice.

A different and perhaps more important aspect of training is that of circle leadership. In this segment such topics as the following are explored: the process and dynamics of group interaction, techniques for building effective teams, goal setting in groups, creativity and synergy in a team, consensual decision making and problem solving, and resolving group conflict.

It is essential to keep in mind that leadership of a quality circle is not the same as supervisory leadership of a work team. Supervising, directing, giving orders, and other controlling behaviors do not apply. The lines of authority should evaporate in the interaction of the members of the circle. The leader is simply a member with special responsibilities.

Social scientists who study leadership have come to some agreement that every supervisor develops and adheres fairly closely to a style of leadership that is the result of work experience as well as deeply held beliefs about the nature of people and the value of the task at hand. Once a style has been established, a great effort is required to change the associated behaviors because they make sense to the supervisor.

Quality circles demand a special style of leadership that is uncommon in America. It is not too likely that the participants in leader training will be prepared for what they are to experience as circle leaders. Those who are used to overseeing their employees closely as well as those who take a more laissez-faire stance will feel somewhat "schizophrenic" in their new circle duties. Thus, some role negotiation should take place in the course of leadership training and in the first few circle sessions. In the course of their training, the leaders can view a live or videotaped demonstration of the proper conduct of a circle. They can also be encouraged to discuss their feelings about nondirective leadership. In each circle an open discussion of the leader role helps to ease any anxiety about what is expected both from the leader and from the members.

The final aspect of leader training is concerned with the administration of the circle. Paperwork required by the structure and other miscellaneous duties are presented. One of these duties involves the minutes that should be kept of every circle session as an historical record of the group's progress. The minutes are usually written by a circle recorder on a standardized, one-page form. These notes along with any other cor- respondence, memoranda, publications, and so forth should be collected by the leader and maintained in an organized, easily accessible format.

The leader must also be informed of his or her responsibility for reporting circle activities and successes to the proper communication channels in the organization and for obtaining the assistance of resource people when needed for circle projects.

Facilitator

Like the circle members and leaders, the facilitator must have a comprehensive understanding of the applications of the basic tools. In addition, he or she must have the ability to facilitate the circle process and presentations to management, expertise in training and training design because he or she will train all leaders, and administrative skills.

Most circle facilitators are trained externally, usually in seminars offered by QC consulting firms and associations. If the organization intends to have several people serving as facilitators, a cost-effective alternative is to develop and offer this training internally. Such a training program should include the following topics:

- The QC concept;
- The company's strategic plan;
- The motivational basis of quality circles;
- Quality-circle structure;
- Basic and advanced tools for QCs;
- Training leaders and members;
- The roles of the facilitator and others;
- Administering a QC system;
- Upgrading and expanding training;
- Arranging presentations to management;
- Consulting with circles; and
- Expanding the circle system.

Because of the volume of learning required of the facilitator, this is the most extensive of the trainings described in this section.

A special skill to be developed is that of consultation, which is the facilitator's major responsibility as the circles expand and stabilize in the organization. As explained in greater detail in the section entitled "Participants," the facilitator is continually "on call" to the circles to assist them in various ways. Some types of assistance are technical in nature, such as clarifying the use of a statistical tool or helping in the design of a presentation to management. Others are quite nontechnical, such as locating and buying materials or soliciting the help of a resource person.

However, the most complex and frequently needed type of assistance provided by the facilitator is that of aiding the circles in dealing with problems of process and interpersonal relations. A skilled facilitator is able to "read between the lines" when difficult situations arise. As long as people work and think together in quality circles or any other kind of group, conflicts will develop. The circle facilitator must be trained in the techniques of managing conflict, but skill in this area is not all that is required. If the facilitator is not accepted as a process expert or trusted in this role, success will be limited. This is the crux of facilitator training: teaching the individual how to function competently as a process expert and not as an authority, so that his or her role is seen by circle members as legitimate and necessary.

Middle Managers

The learning process involved for middle managers who have circles functioning in their areas is one of developing an understanding of QCs and generating a supportive attitude toward circle progress. It is surprising that most QC training programs in user companies have, for the most part, ignored this particular group of people. Perhaps this is why middle managers are so resistant to the change that quality circles symbolize. When a circle fails in an organization, much of the cause can be traced directly to the area's manager.

In order to avoid sabotage by middle management, the authors suggest a biannual session of approximately two hours in length. This session should be designed to update managers on quality-circle activities, to review briefly the purpose and objectives for initiating the program, and to allow plenty of time for those in attendance to voice concerns and raise questions. Training may also be conducted in the skills required to operate an area that has quality circles and to give support to those circles.

PARTICIPANTS

The people involved in this step depend partially on the organization's choice of a training approach. If the company is purchasing an off-the-shelf package, the source of that package must be involved. The authors have worked with companies that have invested money in the materials offered by consulting firms in the QC business, but have not seen the need to buy the expertise of the designer of these materials. This can be a costly mistake unless the organization has the internal capacity to utilize the ideas and concepts presented in an appropriate way. Only someone who is thoroughly familiar with the material and its application in the training setting can give the best advice as to how it can be modified to meet the company's needs.

If the organization has a training department, its personnel should be involved in this step. This approach not only taps the skills and knowledge that these people have to offer; it also minimizes the impact of the perceived threat to internal trainers that is inherent in the process of employing external professionals.

The QC facilitator is responsible for the training of all circle leaders. The leaders themselves are the area managers or supervisors who volunteered in Step 3 after the design team's "sales" presentation. The authors suggest that the leader-training session include as participants not only those who will lead the circles, but also the steering-committee members, internal trainers, quality-control people, and the managers to whom the circle leaders directly report.

The training of circle members is usually different from the collective training of company leaders and facilitators. The members of each circle are trained by their leader in the very context of the circle. The authors have found that this "learning-by-doing" approach is the most effective in providing a circle with a positive beginning.

If the company opts to design its own training, it is a good idea to hire a training-design expert. Although the authors believe that QC training is most effective when delivered by an internal source, they also feel that a training consultant can offer objective and innovative ideas and suggestions to professionalize the program.

TIME FRAME

Depending on the organization's chosen approach to training, it is essential to allow a sufficient amount of time either to become familiar with the purchased package and make all necessary modifications or to do a complete and professional job of designing a customized program. The minimum time for accomplishing either task is eight weeks.

Because each group is trained separately, various time frames should be allowed. Facilitators require from six to ten days of instruction, whereas leaders can learn the necessary skills and concepts in three to five full-day sessions. Members, who learn as they attend their circle meetings, should be allowed no fewer than eight sessions to learn to use the basic tools. At the end of the training meetings, the circles can begin to solve problems, reduce costs, and develop innovations for the company.

TIPS FOR SUCCESS

Because training is so basic to the realization of the QC concept, it is impossible to overemphasize the importance of making the most of this step. The following suggestions will help.

- Check the library for specific information on QC tools. Look under "statistics" or "quality control" to start. Because these tools are not generally discussed in connection with quality circles, it is advisable to ask a librarian for assistance.
- Do not scrimp on training for anyone.
- Be flexible in gauging time requirements. A training module for members does not always equal a single session; some are completed in less than an hour, and some take more time.
- Place an equal emphasis on the development of a cohesive training group and the transfer of knowledge.
- Allow each circle leader to adapt the member-training outline to his or her unique situation.
- Use audiovisuals. They are exceptionally effective learning tools.
- Use internal examples when presenting a tool or technique.
- Make sure that the training program requires the learners to apply their newly learned tools to real problems.
- Discuss the training program in detail with a group of internal people who can objectively evaluate it before it is implemented.

REFERENCE

Slaybough, C.J. Pareto's Law and modern management. *Price Waterhouse Review*, 2(4), 27.

Circle Implementation

OVERVIEW

Step 7 concerns the leap that every circle takes into the reality of everyday innovation, problem solving, and cost savings. These three areas become the focal points of work, at least during the first year or so of the circle's life. In the "Content" section of this step, each of these three important targets is explained in detail.

Also discussed in the "Content" section are the procedures suggested for the establishment of goals and the writing of charters, which provide valuable direction to the circle. Goals are specific statements of achievements that the circle hopes to accomplish. Normally these are in the form of cost savings, time savings, materiel conservation, and profit generation. The writing of objectives does not in any way limit the circle to the accomplishment of what is on paper. The circle will be involved in any number of projects, some related to its objectives and some not. However, these written targets formalize a commitment to the achievement of certain measurable minimums. Anything above and beyond these provides further motivation.

A secondary but valuable purpose of writing objectives is to provide a guide by which to chart progress. Everyone involved in a QC program, from member to senior manager, will want to know how the circles are doing from time to time. A comparison of written objectives with actual achievements provides the data with which to gauge progress.

Finally, these objectives become useful in the project-generation stage of circle work. The circle members occasionally engage in brainstorming to come up with areas that represent unnecessary costs, quality or productivity problems, and innovative possibilities. Through the project-development process learned by the members, the resulting lists are analyzed to determine top priorities that also are of interest to the circle.

These matters are then treated with the appropriate QC tools. When the members are brainstorming these lists, the objectives are useful as thought stimulators. For instance, if the circle has targeted the reduction of department costs for paperwork and this target is in view of the brainstormers, it is highly likely that an idea will be generated that will help in the achievement of that goal.

Circle charters are less concerned with measurement and accomplishment than with group norms, which are the unspoken, psychological agreements among group members that designate appropriate behaviors. These behaviors are not necessarily positive; they may be negative or neutral. The important point is that no group can exist long without them.

Many controls, some overt and others more subtle, are continually exerted on group members. For example, if a group has established a norm that allows its members simply to speak out when they have ideas to contribute, the individual who violates this norm by raising a hand and waiting to be recognized may receive some disapproving or puzzled looks. Thus, the authors have found it to be an extremely valuable experience for circle members to discuss the concept of norms and to identify those that will contribute to the success of their mission.

In summary, Step 7 consists of the series of weekly meetings that circle members attend to review previous learnings and engage in advanced training; to apply statistical techniques and methods to the solving of problems, the reduction of costs, and the generation of innovative ideas in consecutive circle projects; to establish and publish in either written or verbal form a roster of norms for circle membership; and to set measurable, specific goals for circle accomplishment.

CONTENT

For the sake of clarity, let us assume that the leader of a pilot circle has just completed a series of training sessions that ended with a well-received presentation to management. Ahead lies a full year's schedule of weekly one-hour meetings for which there is no agenda. How the leader proceeds depends on the personalities and needs of the members of the circle, but there are some general guidelines to follow session by session. If the first eight sessions have been used for training, as recommended, the agendas for the ninth and tenth sessions might be similar to those presented in Figures 23 and 24, respectively.

Agenda for Session 9

Time	Activity
5 minutes	Administrative details Introduce guests Review the minutes of Session 8
15 minutes	Lecturette on group norms Brainstorm possible positive and negative norms for the circle
5 minutes	Lecturette on the purpose of circle goals and the process of creating them
15 minutes	Write circle goals for this year
15 minutes	Brainstorm possible projects and select Project No. 1
5 minutes	Reactions to the session and assignments

Figure 23. Sample Agenda for the First Post-Training Circle Meeting

---

Agenda for Session 10

Time	
5 minutes	Administrative details Introduce guests Review the minutes of Session 9
15 minutes	Write circle charter from suggestions contributed by members
30 minutes	Work on Project No. 1
10 minutes	Review of the session and assignments

Figure 24. Sample Agenda for the Second Post-Training Circle Meeting

---

A quick look at the sample agendas shows that very little time needs to be spent creating a set of goals and a charter, two crucial tools that will save both time and money as the circle progresses. By the end of these two sessions, the circle will already be delving into the task of solving work problems.

The setting of goals to be accomplished is one of the most misunderstood processes in circle work. The ability to establish future goals is an important life skill. From the moment of birth, each of us has an undetermined amount of time with which to accomplish aspirations. It is a tragedy that so many people reach the end of their lives with the vague feeling that they could have accomplished more if they had tried. Usually, though, the crux of the matter is a lack of direction rather than a failure to try. Specific goals and objectives provide an individual with direction, and the same is true for circles.

To determine whether the circle's goals are viable, the following questions should be answered for each:

- Is the goal *achievable?* Is it something that is within the capabilities of the circle? Does it represent an objective that is neither an insufficient challenge nor an impossibility?

- Is the goal *believable?* Will the circle members and anyone else who reviews the goal find it worthy of consideration? Has the circle avoided trivialities and items of low cost-benefit ratio?

- Is the goal *conceivable?* Is it written so that anyone—even a stranger to the circle—can form a visual image of what is to be accomplished?

It should be noted that *conceivability* has much to do with the form of the goal and, if met, will assure the measurability of the circle's efforts.

A useful model for writing circle objectives is presented in the following equation: The accomplishment of a *specific action* (stated as the infinitive form of a verb, *to . . .*) + the *measurable result* being sought + the *target date* + the *maximum cost* (optional) = the *circle objective*. The following list consists of goals taken from existing circles, most of which conform approximately to this formula.

- To reduce operating expenses by $30 per day through cost-saving ideas and suggestions by November 15;

- To save an amount of time in the production process equal to the amount of time spent in circle meetings by July 20;

- To develop a minimum of five new work techniques and implement them by October 1;

- To reduce by 20 percent the work absenteeism of circle members by August 7;

- To develop a system that will reduce the number of memoranda generated by 50 percent and to install this system by May 25;

- To reduce customer complaints regarding product quality by 75 percent no later than January 1; and
- To engage in ten cost-saving projects, eight problem-solving projects, and one innovative project within the next one-year period ending September 15.

If they are met, goals such as these result in attractive payoffs for the companies involved. The accomplishment of such goals also provides a great deal of satisfaction and a sense of achievement for circle members. Still another bonus is the fact that each goal can be easily measured so that the circle program can be evaluated according to the process presented in Step 8.

Writing the circle charter is a completely different type of task. The charter consists of a series of statements that sound very much like rules. Many of an individual circle's charter statements will be universally held by all circles in the system, but others will be unique to that circle. Charters are meant to be much more general and more lasting than objectives. They have little future emphasis because they focus on the way in which members are expected to behave from the outset. They are, in fact, similar in content to an organization's statement of mission or policy. The authors have borrowed the charter presented in Figure 25 from a circle within a client organization.

Quality-Circle Charter

1. Membership in the circle is completely voluntary.

2. The circle is to meet for one hour each week during normal working hours.

3. The circle consists of a leader, a recorder, and members.

4. All members are to be trained for a minimum of eight hours in the skills they need to operate effectively.

5. The work-place problems that the circle selects to solve are to be limited to those that fall within its area of authority and control.

6. The circle has the authority to call on expert resource people from within the company to help in its efforts at problem solution and cost reduction.

7. The members agree to set goals for achievement for the coming year within three months of circle establishment and to revise these goals on a yearly basis.

8. The circle is authorized to call on the department facilitator at any time for assistance in problem solution.

Figure 25. Sample Charter

9. The circle is authorized to suggest any ideas it has for inclusion in QC training.

10. The members agree to consider any idea suggested by another QC or an outside source that might help the circle in its goal achievement.

11. All suggestions referred to the department facilitator are to be responded to within two weeks. If a response cannot be given at the end of two weeks, the circle is to be notified, the delay explained, and a new date specified for receiving a response.

12. The members agree to arrive on time for all meetings and to complete all assignments in a timely manner.

13. Every member agrees to contribute his or her leadership ability to the circle.

14. Decisions are to be made by consensus, and enough time is to be allowed to discuss all the issues thoroughly.

15. All conflicts that may arise between members or between this circle and others are to be discussed openly.

Figure 25 (continued).

At the beginning of this step, the three general areas of circle intervention were mentioned: cost savings, problem solving, and innovations. The circle members must clearly understand each of these areas so that they can select appropriate projects with realistic expectations and time frames.

With cost-saving projects, the members closely examine various processes, methods, practices, materials, and other items related to the cost of operating their work area. This analysis leads to the implementation of a plan to eliminate or reduce the cost that has been found to be unnecessary or too high. The results of cost-saving projects are less dramatic than those of problem-solving and innovative projects. However, their greatest value is their ongoing nature. Once a problem is solved, it is over; an innovation is also a one-time proposition. But when a cost is reduced or eliminated, the benefits are still accumulating years later. Thus, cost-saving projects have become a favorite of circles in many organizations.

Problem-solving projects are also popular, but for a different reason. Because problem solving is the main process for which the circle members have been trained, the related skills are the first to be used. When the QC movement began, the primary problem focus was on quality. Today, however, circles work on problems ranging from human relations to safety. As stated previously, a problem must be identified as such before any steps can be taken toward solution. Some problems are obvious to the circle members, such as chronically lost files or an oil leak. Others are more hidden, and there are times when these "unseen" problems are brought to the attention of the circle by those outside it. A fellow worker, a manager, or even another circle can uncover problems that represent potential projects.

The type of circle project that offers the most dramatic payoff involves innovations. These are developed only rarely in the life of a circle because they consist of creating something from nothing. In the most fluid and free moments of brainstorming, a member may mention an idea that subsequently evolves into a totally new product or process, perhaps even replacing a product or process that was nonproblematic. If there is enough trust in the company that employees will be kept working, circles may even invent ways to reduce the number of workers required. Innovative projects demand a great deal more creativity, time, and energy than do problem-solving or cost-saving projects, but their psychological and financial rewards are tremendous.

The authors suggest that the circle brainstorm possible projects for each category. Then the members should assign priorities to the items on each separate list, combine the three lists, and reassign priorities to determine projects and project order. Some circles prefer cost-saving projects; others like to alternate for variety. Any order is effective as long as the members clearly understand the differences in the three types.

PARTICIPANTS

The most important people in a QC system are the members of the individual circle and their leader. Their ability to work together is what produces the results desired from the program. Nevertheless, conflicts will arise in the circle relationships as they will in any group. Because the circle is always in need of fine tuning, the role of the circle facilitator is crucial.

The facilitator is the most important member of the support staff for the QC program. This person will be well trained in both the technical and the human aspects of quality circles. Therefore, it is essential to select someone who has excellent human-relations skills to fill this important post. Whether this person is recruited from within the organization or from an external source, he or she must know how to listen and get along well with others of all stations in life.

The actions of the circles and the facilitator are to be guided by the steering committee. This small, heterogeneous group will represent most areas of the company through the participation of senior managers in regular discussion meetings. Just as circle participation is voluntary, so is the contribution of the time of these steering-committee members. The need should be clear for a highly persuasive "sales" presentation to enlist these busy people in policy-making work for the circle system.

Step 7 coordinates everyone's efforts. The steering committee, if the company has one, begins making policy; the facilitator or administrator is answering calls for assistance from the pilot circles and developing new training where needed; the circle leaders are guiding their groups to cohesiveness and effectiveness; and, finally, the circle members are starting to work on the numerous projects that they have developed. In short, the circle program is an operational reality.

TIME FRAME

Because this step begins the ongoing reality of quality circles, there is no specific time frame in which it will be complete. It starts immediately following the training of leaders and members and the orientation of the steering committee. As long as the organization has quality circles, in effect there is no end to Step 7.

On the other hand, the circle projects do have a start and a finish. Some last only a week or two, while others may take as long as six months or more to complete.

TIPS FOR SUCCESS

The following recommendations are offered for this step.

- Encourage each circle to select a relatively simple project for its first attempt. Early success will build the members' confidence and provide quick feedback.
- Invite members of senior management to attend circle meetings to show support and interest.
- Establish a company newsletter on quality circles to let everyone know how they are progressing.
- Arrange for outside publicity, if possible.
- Schedule quarterly meetings for the circle leaders to build a support group, generate new ideas, and solve problems.
- Encourage the circles to invite outside guests to their meetings.
- Monitor the circles closely enough to make sure that they are dealing with appropriate projects.
- Keep careful records of the circle projects in order to avoid duplication or conflict between circles.

- Do not interfere. Watching every move, trying to solve every dispute or problem, criticizing heavily, or providing too much support can lead to circle failure.
- Enjoy the results of circle efforts.

Evaluation and Refinement

OVERVIEW

At this point in the process, an idea has been turned into a working reality, and it is time to measure that reality against the original objectives of the strategic plan. This step begins with a review of the goals created during the strategic-planning session as well as what motivated the organization to implement quality circles. These objectives may be many and varied or few and select. Whatever the case, they must now be evaluated to determine whether or not the QC program has been successful.

Several areas may be addressed in the quality-circle evaluation. One of the major areas, and the one most critical to American business and industry, is that of productivity. "Productivity" is one of the catchwords of the Eighties; it attracts the attention of people in all sectors of the economy and at all levels of an organization. However, there is a problem inherent in seeking productivity improvement: Productivity means different things to different people.

In their consulting work, the authors seek to improve the productivity of the individual, the work group, and the organization. They have found that for each client they must repeat the process of defining what productivity means. Every organizational definition they have encountered has been unique to that organization.

For all practical purposes, however, productivity means doing more for less. If improved productivity is the company's QC goal, then those involved with the project must identify exactly how they define "more" and "less." This defining process should begin at the outset of the efforts to bring QCs into the organization.

In a sense, productivity must be defined by each QC for its own work area. One way to simplify this process is to look at what is ultimately produced. Although all of the tasks performed on the job are important, the final product is what must be measured in order to gauge overall productivity.

The individual circle must first identify its work area's end products. Usually there are fewer than five. Once the circle has determined its products, it can measure the various inputs required to produce them. When this has been accomplished, the members have begun to assess the work area's productivity.

Quality is another area that is usually addressed when evaluating a QC program. Quality circles were originally called "quality-control circles" and were created simply for the purpose of improving the overall quality of manufactured products. Now that QCs have evolved into a technique of change and improvement, quality is just one of the many goals accomplished.

Quality, like productivity, requires a thorough defining process in order to meet the criteria of measurability in program outcomes. In fact, quality is often cited as one factor in the definition of productivity for an organization. The question to be asked, for the purposes of this step, is the following: "Has the overall quality of the product (or service) been improved through the efforts of the quality circles?" The answer will come initially from the quality-control or quality-assurance personnel, then from the circles themselves, and ultimately from the customer. It is the job of the circle to build quality into the product or service, and it is the job of the QC planner to determine how well that has been done.

Several measures can be used to gauge quality. For example, the number of customer complaints or the quantity of scrap can be readily identified. The major point in a QC effort is to have the circle members themselves select the items that they think are the most important to measure. As is the case with productivity, this selection process is important in increasing awareness among the circle members, and awareness and effort lead to improvement.

A third area that may be evaluated is that of employee morale. Although it may not seem to be so, morale is often easier to measure than productivity. Chief indicators of high morale include low levels of absenteeism, turnover, employee theft or sabotage, and filed grievances. Somewhat more difficult to measure, but certainly as valid, is the degree of energy and enthusiasm that employees bring with them to work.

Initial measurements of many of these indicators can be made by checking company records, but the information in these records may not suffice without including the results of a company-wide attitude survey and/or interviews. The better the questions asked, the more valuable the data collected.

Utilization of human resources is another possible area of measurement. This is a fairly new field of study, but it is growing in technique and measurement methodology every day. Basically, if the company has set out to maximize its use of human talent, the first step of the evaluation process is to audit the human resources to determine what is available versus what is being utilized. Then it becomes possible to measure the difference between availability and utilization due to the effect of the circle system.

Many companies are experiencing broad changes in their utilization factors because of quality circles. The explanation is simple: Through the circle process, which incorporates training and visibility, talent can be readily identified. Also, many QCs have alternate leaders who are trained in leadership skills. As these employees mature into capable circle leaders, they also mature into potential managers. Indirectly, QCs in these organizations have evolved into effective vehicles for management development.

Additional areas of circle evaluation may include human relations, safety, management planning, and even community or public relations.

As has been emphasized throughout this book, each quality-circle program, including its evaluation, is a unique system that fits its organization exclusively. The QC planner must decide which measurements will be most reliable and valid and then design measuring devices that are both accurate and easily administered.

There are two purposes for such measuring. In Steps 2 through 4, quality circles were "sold" as a pilot project and a management innovation with which the company could experiment. In order to make the switch from pilot project to way of life, a reselling job needs to be done. Therefore, the first practical purpose of the evaluation is to provide accurate data that support a proposal for QC continuance. These data enable the QC planner to present, in a logical fashion, exactly what the program has achieved.

The second purpose is to validate the implementation

team's efforts. The members of this team have spent considerable time and energy preparing for and implementing quality circles in the organization, and they deserve to know how effective they have been. A well-designed and thorough evaluation provides this information; an opportunity for a valuable learning experience exists in this feedback process.

If the program has been planned well and the authors' model has been closely followed, success has probably resulted. This is not to say that mistakes have not been made; mistakes are inevitable and useful in the revision process suggested in this step. In fact, revision of the QC program is an important by-product of evaluation.

The revision process starts with an examination of the strategic plan that has been closely followed during the installation. In effect, this examination questions whether the plan has been appropriate and effective. It should be remembered that plans are made to be changed; consequently, alterations at this point are perfectly legitimate. The authors suggest that those involved in this process include the members of the implementation team, the steering-committee members, a few circle leaders and members, the QC facilitator(s), and anyone else involved and interested in making improvements. The brainstorm technique can be used to identify the errors that have been made and to analyze what caused them; then solutions can be generated. By using QC tools and techniques, this group can thus smooth out the operation of the system.

CONTENT

The first part of this step, evaluation, can consist of one or more of the following activities:

- Tabulating the number of circle goals deemed accomplished by the members;
- Conducting an attitude survey among participants in the circle program;
- Examining employee records for absenteeism and turnover;
- Analyzing customer-complaint and/or -satisfaction indicators;
- Determining cost savings versus the start-up cost for the QC program;

- Conducting "sensing" interviews with key personnel to determine the receptivity toward QCs in the company;
- Measuring the numerous productivity factors;
- Recruiting new volunteers to join the QC movement in the company; and
- Requesting reports from the quality-control department.

This is merely a partial list of ways to evaluate the program. The specific objectives involved provide the best clues as to which to use.

The information gathered in this evaluation supplies indicators of where and how revisions are to be accomplished. The changes to be made may be simple ones, such as a rescheduling of additional circles. On the other hand, it may become necessary to revamp the entire plan and the program that was created from it. Those responsible for evaluation should not be discouraged if a lot of redesign work results from the examination of data; the program will certainly be improved because of these efforts.

When deciding on alterations to the program, the areas to which careful attention should be given include the following:

- The expansion time schedule;
- Training design and materials;
- Structure of power and authority;
- Vehicles for communication among circles and between circles and management;
- The size and make-up of the administrative staff for QCs;
- The procedures for selecting circle members and leaders;
- Areas into which the circles may delve;
- The content of circle goals and objectives;
- The process for determining projects;
- The QC reporting and/or presentation process;
- Recognition and reward procedures; and
- Advanced training and development.

PARTICIPANTS

Among those to be included in the process of evaluation and revision may be a consultant who can provide an objective view of the program. If the expertise of a QC consultant has been utilized during the installation, this individual should certainly be required to evaluate the work performed. If the organization has designed and implemented its own program, it is advisable at this time to consider calling in a professional who specializes in quality circles or in program evaluation; either type of specialist will be able to do a more objective job of assessment than can be accomplished internally.

Certain key personnel should also be involved. These might include the company facilitator(s), steering-committee and/or senior-management members, prominent circle leaders and members, and the members of the implementation team. All can play a useful role in evaluating the success of the quality circles.

TIME FRAME

Results would be inconclusive if a formal evaluation were to be conducted before allowing the fully trained pilot circles to operate for at least six months. This provides a sufficient amount of time for the participants to become familiar with the "ins" and "outs" of circle life and, thus, to develop a stable and individual character within each QC. A six-month period also permits the circles to make measurable progress toward their goals and allows all of those involved to become comfortable with their roles and with each other.

An in-depth study of the impact of quality circles on the organization consumes approximately six weeks. During this period of research, survey taking, productivity measuring, data analysis, conclusion drawing, and other evaluative activities, the circles continue to progress. There is no reason to interrupt their functioning and every reason to encourage them to keep working on their goals.

The time frame for the revision stage of this step varies greatly from company to company. The number and type of revisions made and the time required to complete them are the products of the analysis. However, it should be assumed that revisions are an ongoing process that will continue as long as the quality-circle program exists.

TIPS FOR SUCCESS

Total success for the QC program is finally at hand with this step. It is important to proceed with caution and to make note of the following tips.

- Do not conduct a formal evaluation before the pilot circles have had a minimum of six months to become established and functional.

- To supplement the evaluation, be alert to any comments made about the program. Listening skills are particularly valuable at this point.
- Do not overreact to conditions or situations that are initially determined to be problems. Almost any trouble with the program can be corrected with thought and patience.
- Do not rush into problem solving until every problem encountered has been analyzed to determine its logical cause.
- Do not be afraid to disband, at least temporarily, a circle that has begun badly.
- Consider suggesting a system of alternating or revolving leadership within the pilot circles.
- Consider deviations from standard QC procedures as project suggestions are made by the steering committee and/or the area managers.
- If part of the revision necessitates retraining, be sure that the training program itself is revised.
- Determine a cost-benefit ratio. Nothing will better convince senior management of the value of QCs.
- Make certain that managers—not the members of the evaluation team—present the results and recommendations to top-level executives.
- As revisions are made, keep in mind that success is a journey rather than a destination.

Expansion

OVERVIEW

The expansion of a quality-circle program continues slowly but surely until the system permeates the entire organization. Only a few words need to be said about expansion; in effect, the QC planner is the real author of this step.

Expansion is the systematic addition of new circles to the program by engaging in the basic activities of Steps 5 through 8. The leaders and members of these new circles are drawn from the volunteer list developed during the process of "selling" QCs to middle and line management. If it is necessary to increase this list, the "sales" presentation should be repeated, this time with supporting data from the evaluation.

The expansion phase has plenty of room for innovations, examples of which are as follows:

- *"Co-circles" (two or more circles joined together for a project);*
- *"Mini-circles" (small groups consisting of a few members of a circle working on a project of their own);*
- *Management circles (those whose members are middle or senior managers within a division); and*
- *Intra-organizational circles (those including representatives from all areas of the company who work on problems that affect the organization as a whole).*

Steering committees are often assigned the task of being the creative force behind these innovations, which are best approached with a brainstorming session to raise organizational possibilities.

CONTENT

Essentially, this step repeats Steps 5 through 8 with the omission of the orientation toward a pilot program. By this time quality circles have proven themselves, been smoothed over, and become a way of life in the organization; they are an operational reality.

In the progression toward an organization-wide circle system, the company will be adding two to five new circles per month, following the same procedure for qualifying each new group that was used for qualifying the original pilots. All training should be scheduled on a regular basis, and advanced training for the experienced circles may begin.

PARTICIPANTS

During expansion all of those involved in the program actively play their roles. The steering committee continues to establish policy and review practice; the facilitators help new circles to begin; the leaders train their circles, organize them, and help them to start on projects; and the members learn tools and techniques and begin to use them to solve problems in their work areas.

Newcomers to the operation are managers or supervisors who volunteer their areas for circles and the employees who become members. Although these potential circles must meet the criteria established for the program, the order in which they are added is not important. It is best to arrange training sessions so that both production and staff members attend. In this way the trainees receive a well-rounded circle education as opposed to the narrow focus that may result from limiting attendance to one type of employee or the other.

TIME FRAME

As stated previously, the addition of two to five new circles per month is enough for any system to handle. Each new circle should be allowed six months to become organized before its accomplishments are evaluated.

A strong foundation has been laid for the company's QC program. Approximately ten to twelve months have passed, and it will probably be another three to five years before the "infancy" stage is complete. The road to quality-circle maturity is paved with learning, excitement, and individual and organizational growth. The authors extend their wishes for a successful journey.

TIPS FOR SUCCESS

The following are a few tips for the successful expansion of a QC program.

- Involve senior managers in the expansion process.
- Be prepared to handle (and not be swayed by) pressure to expand rapidly, which can be expected if the pilot project has been a success.
- Develop a schedule of training and circle additions for the next six to eighteen months so that volunteers know what to expect.
- Invite experienced circle leaders to participate in the training sessions and orientation sessions. They have valuable expertise to contribute.
- Contact and establish an information network with other local organizations using or considering quality circles.
- Consider an organizational QC conference during which the circles can display their project results.

APPENDIX

Bibliography

SUGGESTED BOOKS

Adler, M.J. *Aristotle for everybody*. New York: Macmillan, 1978.

American Society for Quality Control. *Quality control circles: Applications, tools, and theory*, 1979. (Available from Department PI 800, 161 West Wisconsin Avenue, Milwaukee, WI 53203.)

Blake, R.R., & Mouton, J.S. *Productivity: The human side*. New York: AMACOM, 1981.

Cole, R.E. *Work, mobility and participation: A comparative study of American and Japanese industry*. Berkeley: University of California Press, 1979.

Dewar, D.L. *Quality circles: Answers to 100 frequently asked questions*. Red Bluff, CA: Dewar Associates, 1979. (Available from Dewar Associates, 234 South Main Street, Red Bluff, CA 96080.)

Dewar, D.L., & Beardsley, J.F. *Quality circles*. Red Bluff, CA: International Association of Quality Circles, 1979.

Fuller, R.B. *Synergetics 2*. New York: Macmillan, 1979.

Fulmer, R.M. *The new management*. New York: Macmillan, 1974.

Gellerman, S.W. *Gellerman on motivation and productivity*. San Diego, CA: University Associates, 1973. (Tape package.)

Juran, J.M. (Ed.). *Quality control handbook* (3rd ed.). New York: McGraw-Hill, 1974.

Shaw, M.E. *Group dynamics: The psychology of small group behavior*. New York: McGraw-Hill, 1971.

Zukov, G. *The dancing Wu Li masters*. New York: William Morrow, 1979.

SUGGESTED ARTICLES

Burck, C.S. Working smarter. *Fortune*, June 15, 1981, pp. 61-73.

Cole, R.E. Made in Japan: A spur to U.S. productivity. *ASIA Magazine*, May/June 1979, p. 76.

Gibson, P. Short term fad or long term fundamental? *The Quality Circles Journal*, May 1981, pp. 25-27.

Metz, E.J. Caution: Quality circles ahead. *Training and Development Journal,* August 1981, pp. 71-76.

Nelson, J. Quality circles become contagious. *Industry Week,* April 14, 1980, p. 103.

Pascarella, P. Humanagement at Honeywell. *Industry Week,* July 27, 1981, pp. 33-36.

Rendall, E. QC's—A third wave intervention. *Training and Development Journal,* March 1981, pp. 28-31.

Schleicher, W.F. Quality circles: The participative team approach. *Quality Magazine,* October 1981, pp. 28-31.

Sullivan, S.J. Can the effectiveness of QC circles be measured? *The Quality Circles Journal,* May 1981, pp. 29-31.

Yager, E.G. The QCC explosion. *Training and Development Journal,* April 1981, pp. 98-105.

Zemke, R. Quality circles: Using pooled effort to promote excellence. *Training,* August 1980, pp. 30-31.

Zemke, R. Honeywell imports QC's as a long term management strategy. *Training,* August 1980, pp. 91-94.